PAY FOR COLLEGE

WITHOUT GOING BROKE

FUND YOUR CHILD'S EDUCATION BY UNLOCKING *FREE* MONEY

Perry De Fontaine, CPA

R^ethink

First published in Great Britain in 2024
by Rethink Press (www.rethinkpress.com)

© Copyright Perry De Fontaine

All rights reserved. No part of this publication may be reproduced, stored in, or introduced into a retrieval system, or transmitted, in any form, or by any means (electronic, mechanical, photocopying, recording, or otherwise) without the prior written permission of the publisher.

The right of Perry De Fontaine to be identified as the author of this work has been asserted by him in accordance with the Copyright, Designs, and Patents Act 1988.

This book is sold subject to the condition that it shall not, by way of trade or otherwise, be lent, resold, hired out, or otherwise circulated without the publisher's prior consent in any form of binding or cover other than that in which it is published and without a similar condition including this condition being imposed on the subsequent purchaser.

Cover image © iStock | skynesher

Disclaimer: The financial ideas discussed in this book should never be used without first assessing your own financial situation and consulting a qualified financial adviser. Neither the author nor the publisher can be held responsible for any losses that may result from financial decisions made after reading this book.

For my wife, Angie, and our son, Adrien
— thank you for all your love and support

Contents

Introduction

If you believe college is beyond your financial means, you might wonder whether there is any possibility of educating your kids to this level. With costs rapidly rising, college can seem elusive to many, causing more and more families to question the value of a degree. In addition, the US college system can be complicated and confusing. You might not believe you can afford college, or you may think that school choices are limited by sticker price, leaving students to try to get their degrees the hard way. You might even be willing to spend all your savings or borrow $40–50K+ per year for the sake of your kids' education. The frustration that began fifty years ago when I was in high school is still evident today.

Wouldn't it be great to be able to send your kids to schools you never thought you could afford? Wouldn't you prefer *not* to be in debt, or to save your money for your child's grad school—if not for your other kids' future college funds? Wouldn't you like to hang on to your savings for your retirement? Let me assure you that these possibilities are all within your reach.

Did you know, no matter what your financial situation, you can get tens of thousands of dollars per year in *free* money for college education? What is particularly amazing is that most of this financial aid comes from the colleges themselves, not (as you might expect) from the government or private scholarships. The average amount of free money that private colleges provide, on an annual basis, is close to $20K; however, many colleges routinely provide much more ($30–60K+ per year). Also, 82% of first year students at those schools receive free money from the schools themselves.[1] This book is packed with insights designed to enable you to access that cash so that you are able to make those choices for yourself.

People routinely ask me why I am so passionate about college planning. Quite simply, finding the means to pay for college education has not improved since I was in high school. I was the first in my family to ever

---

1   J Ma and M Pender, "Trends in college pricing and student aid, 2021," (CollegeBoard, 2021), https://research.collegeboard.org/media/pdf/trends-college-pricing-student-aid-2021.pdf, accessed 7 September 2023

consider going to college. We had no money, and the local high school provided no financial advice. I didn't know how to pay for college and was faced with the reality of not going. I had to figure it out on my own, but I was determined to find a way. Thus began my seven-year journey to get a four-year degree.

If I had not ultimately discovered the magic of other people's money (in the form of financial aid from the colleges themselves), who knows whether I would have ever finished college. I am eternally grateful that I discovered how the system worked, which enabled me to graduate from a great college and go on to build a successful career. I am now a certified public accountant (CPA) with more than forty years of financial services industry experience, helping multibillion-dollar companies with their money, including as an executive with major consulting and Wall Street firms advising Fortune 500 clients.

About twenty years ago I decided that, instead of focusing on companies, I wanted to give back to my community by helping individuals and families with their finances, so I joined up with a friend and neighbor's local tax, investment, and financial planning firm. Because of my background, I added securities and insurance licensing to my CPA license, and thus began helping clients with their finances. After starting this transition, I soon discovered that one of the major issues facing parents was the high—and rapidly increasing—cost of college. In addition, I was shocked by the lack of readily available information to help parents with this problem. Based on what I had learned from my own college journey—most importantly how to access free money—I decided to share my knowledge with others in the community. Unfortunately, this lack of knowledge still exists today.

My passion is for the kids. Over the years it has been rewarding to have helped so many get to great schools their families could never have afforded otherwise. I have been frustrated at not being able to help more families because there are only so many people I can reach through public speaking in my community, at local high schools, and through referrals, which is why I've written this book. Over the next few chapters I am going to educate you about what I call the Ideal Approach. What you will discover is that most free money comes from the colleges themselves, and to access that money you must find the right schools, solving the matrix for your unique college situation.

I'm here to help you get over those seemingly impenetrable hurdles. No child that wants to go to college should be denied the opportunity because their parents are unaware of funding. Whatever your financial situation, I aim to show each and every one of you how to make college more affordable, opening the door to colleges you never thought your student would be in a position to attend, and so creating future possibilities you didn't believe were possible.

PART ONE
LET'S GET EDUCATED

1
College Costs

Did you know that four years at college can typically cost $100–300K per child, if not more?

It's expensive, no matter where you go

I'm not just talking about tuition fees. There are books to buy, room and board to pay for, living expenses… as well as all those out-of-pocket overheads involved in living on campus, including basics such as toothpaste, laundry detergent—and let's not forget the occasional pizza. All of this mounts up to a typical college cost over four years of $100–300K—and that's just for one child.

Take a look at the following figures:[2]

Annual college costs

Average public IS university	$27,300
Average public OOS university	$44,200
Average private university	$55,800
Elite private university	$80,000+

IS: in-state; OOS: out-of-state. Costs include everything (all the basics I've mentioned above).

These are national averages, which means prices in individual states could be even higher:

Estimated costs for colleges in New Jersey, 2023[3]

IS public	$35,000
OOS public	$55,000
Private	$65,000–80,000+

IS: in-state; OOS: out-of-state.

It hasn't taken long to establish that college education is expensive, no matter where your kid goes. But there's more. What happens if you have more than one child with college ambitions? And let's not forget that college costs keep going up. In the last twenty years, the average tuition and fee costs of four-year

---

2   J Ma and M Pender, "Trends in college pricing and student aid, 2021," (CollegeBoard, 2021), https://research.collegeboard.org/media/pdf/trends-college-pricing-student-aid-2021.pdf, accessed 7 September 2023

3   Based on first-hand knowledge of the author

public schools have increased by 88%, and four-year private schools are up by 44%.[4]

You also need to recognize that you are paying these college fees with "after-tax" dollars. This hypothetical example based on one child in college brings home this point:

Paying for college with after-tax dollars

Federal tax bracket	Public $140,000	Private $220,000	Elite private $320,000
12%	$159,100	$250,000	$363,600
22%	$179,500	$282,100	$410,300
32%	$205,900	$323,500	$470,600

This hypothetical example is for illustration purposes only. Actual results may vary.

Money for college bills will come from net after-tax dollars. To come up with, for example, $140,000 over four years for a public school ($35,000/year), you would have to earn $159,100 "pre-tax," then pay federal taxes, in order to be left with $140,000 available to pay college bills. If you are in the 32% tax bracket, you need to earn $205,900 to come up with the same $140,000 after federal taxes. How many of you have that *extra* money available after paying all of your regular bills? I thought so. This brings home the fact that, for the vast majority, your income alone will not fund your kids' college bills.

---

4   J Ma and M Pender, "Trends in college pricing and student aid, 2021"

Options for paying college fees

Savings

How many of you have saved all that money? Don't feel bad; you are not alone. Did you know that almost 35% of all parents are not saving for college in any way, and those that have, only saved an average of about $18K?[5]

Borrowing

How much do you think you can borrow, and from where? Do you borrow against your home (refinance or get a home equity loan/line) or beg the bank for a personal loan? Do you pile it onto credit cards? Are there student or college loans?

How many of you are even willing to borrow that kind of money?

Scholarships

Do you think there are enough college merit scholarships or private scholarships out there to cover these costs?

---

5   A Nova, "Parents have on average $18,000 saved for college, and that's still not nearly enough," *CNBC* (18 May 2018), https://cnbc.com/2018/05/18/parents-have-on-average-18000-saved-for-college-and-thats-still-not-nearly-enough.html, accessed 7 September 2023

Sadly, most people get scared off by college sticker prices and simply do not believe they can afford college. They tend to either:

- Go for the cheapest option they can find—what I call "going the hard way" (like I did). Typically, that means living at home and commuting somewhere locally.

- Or, worse still, they don't go to college at all.

I am here to tell you, right now, that neither of these options is right for any child that wants to go to college. A college education is an investment in your child's future and is attainable. It should be on your radar. The key is learning how to access free (other people's) money. Wouldn't it be at least worth keeping the door open by learning what is possible?

Summary

Yes, college education is expensive, but do not be put off by the cost. Do not feel you need to drain your bank account, borrow against your home or credit cards, or look for a suitable scholarship that might not exist. Don't fall into the trap of looking for the cheapest option or avoiding college for your child altogether. This book will show you how you can send your child to the right school without going into debt or spending your life savings.

2
Is College Worth It?

Did you know a college education statistically improves quality of life?

Investing in the future

Because of the costs, especially in recent years, many families are questioning the value of a college education. Is attaining higher education worth it?

Unequivocally, the answer is "yes." College is an investment in your child's future, not simply an expense.

Not convinced? Check out these numbers, which indicate earning potential based on education and qualifications:

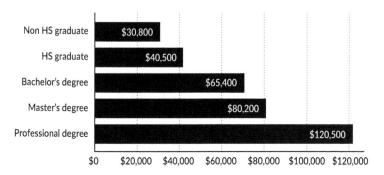

Median earnings of full-time workers, age 25+,
by education level, 2019.[6]

In addition to the economic return on investment (ROI), college grads typically provide more benefits to society (public benefit). For example, college grads:

- Pay more in taxes

- Need less public support

- Volunteer and vote more

- Are healthier and smoke less[7]

6   J Ma, M Pender, and M Welch, "Education pays, 2019: The benefits of higher education for individuals and society," (CollegeBoard, 2019), https://research.collegeboard.org/media/pdf/education-pays-2019-full-report.pdf, accessed 11 September 2023

7   J Ma, M Pender, and M Welch, "Education pays, 2019"

Assuming you agree college is an investment and is worth it, wouldn't it be great if we could get lots of free money and make it less costly?

My personal college journey

I want to tell you about my situation in high school. Based on costs, four-year colleges were out of the picture. I figured my only opportunity was to live at home and commute to a community/county two-year college. It was only years later I came to realize that this was going the hard way.

I lived in a portion of New Jersey (NJ) where, at the time, the closest community college was twenty-five miles away. I had no car, and where I lived (the early 1970s version of *Jersey Shore*), jobs for kids were scarce. My means of transportation at the time was hitchhiking.

Through research, I discovered that because I was born in California (Los Angeles), if I returned before I turned eighteen, I could get a four-year public college tuition for free. That just left me with finding somewhere to live.

My parents divorced when I was young, and my mom eventually moved me and my siblings back to NJ where she had family. At the time, I was twelve years old.

My father remained in California, so I moved in with him at the age of seventeen. This wasn't easy. He had remarried and had a two-year-old son. The deal was I could live there, but I had to pay rent and pay for everything else on my own. The good news was there were lots of jobs available locally. I applied to the closest four-year college to where my father lived, was accepted, and was on a plane to California a week after my NJ high school graduation.

My college decision was based solely on sticker price and the practical options available to me. If I had not been presented with this California opportunity, I highly doubt I would have stuck with the NJ county college option; in fact, none of my high school friends that were in similar financial situations and tried that route ever finished college. I was fortunate to have another option.

A life-changing turning point

My California option had a number of challenges. In terms of work, my jobs included delivering the *Los Angeles Times* seven mornings a week, plus working a graveyard shift at a local gas station. Once college started, I realized I was attending a school where I did not feel challenged. It was not the right school for me.

On the plus side, I started meeting other students, including those who lived in the dorms on campus. When they discovered I was working these jobs and commuting, they wondered why. My short answer was: "How else can I pay the college bills, plus food and board?" Some had parents that could pay the bills, but many others with no money like me said they were receiving financial aid—including lots of *free* money. Hard as it is to believe now, at the time I had never heard of such "financial aid."

The impact of that knowledge was life changing. Because of what I discovered, two years later I transferred to a prestigious school in NJ, received lots of free financial aid, lived on campus, and graduated.

Prepare to be surprised

Not only do few people accumulate sufficient dollars dedicated to college funds, most believe they earn too much to be eligible for financial aid. Also— and I'll keep stressing this throughout the book—you can get other people's money to pay for college. No matter what your financial situation is, you can get thousands—even tens of thousands—in *free* money per year.

Did you know that private schools with the big, scary sticker prices can be less expensive than cheaper in-state public schools? Surprised? I thought you might be. Take a look at a few other facts; at least some of which, I guarantee, will be news to you:

- 22% of US households have kids under 18 (73 million);[8] and of 2.7 million high school graduates in 2021, about 62% attend college (43% go to four-year schools; 19% attend two-year schools). [9]

- Most people that start college go the hard way (living at home and commuting), yet the best chance for college success is living on campus at your four-year right school.

- The key is to find the right school for your unique situation—solve your unique matrix.

- Most free money for college comes from the colleges themselves, not from the government or private scholarships.

- Sticker prices don't matter—what matters is true cost (after free financial aid). Bear in mind that some schools have more money than others.

- 82% of kids attending private schools receive at least some free financial aid. Plus, the average discount is 33% off the total price.[10]

---

8   United States Census Bureau, "Age and sex composition in the United States: 2021," (2021), https://census.gov/data/tables/2021/demo/age-and-sex/2021-age-sex-composition.html, accessed 7 September 2023

9   National Center for Education Statistics (NCES), "Fast facts: Immediate transition to college," https://nces.ed.gov/fastfacts/display.asp?id=51, accessed 7 September 2023

10   J Ma and M Pender, "Trends in college pricing and student aid, 2021," (CollegeBoard, 2021), https://research.collegeboard.org/media/pdf/trends-college-pricing-student-aid-2021.pdf, accessed 7 September 2023

- Colleges are the gatekeepers to the vast majority of financial aid (including college loans). To get access, you must ask for it (by completing financial aid forms). Most parents think the Free Application for Federal Student Aid (FAFSA) is the only financial aid form needed, but the majority of the schools with the most free money require more financial aid forms than just the FAFSA.

- The more free money you get, the less you have to pay and/or borrow. More free money for undergrad saves more for grad school, more free money for your other kids, and more free money for you and your retirement.

Competition for college admissions is increasing

How do you get into your college of choice? Competition is fierce and getting worse. For example:

- Many of our top schools (the top 50–60) have acceptance rates of less than 10%, with some less than 5%.[11]

- These rates have trended downward from when I started twenty years ago. The Harvard

---

11   Ivywise, "College acceptance rates," (2023), https://ivywise.com/ivywise-knowledgebase/admission-statistics, accessed 7 September 2023

admittance rate was 9.8% in 2007 and 3.4% in 2023; Columbia was 12.0% in 2007 and 3.9% in 2023; Duke was 21.0% in 2007 and 6.0% in 2023. Even public schools are getting more competitive—The University of Michigan had a 50.3% admittance rate in 2007 and only 17.7% in 2022.[12]

This trend will generally continue, and I expect even more competition going forward. Why? Kids are applying to more schools than before. Because many have gone "SAT optional" (as a result of COVID19), students are not worried about test scores and are applying to more "reach" (where it's harder to get accepted) schools. Further, our population is growing in pure numbers, but the number of colleges and universities have essentially stayed flat.

Do not get discouraged. There are many, many great schools out there—and better yet, with lots of free money.

When to start the college application process

You might think that the fall of senior year in high school is the right time to start the college application process. Sadly, that's when too many do start. Did you know, many college application deadlines are in

---

12   Ivywise, "College acceptance rates"

the fall of senior year? Most are due by 1 January of senior year, even though they don't start school until the following September.

The earlier you start, the more leisurely and less stressful the process will be. The worst thing that can happen is you wait until it's too late to maximize your opportunities for college success.

It's never too early to start planning for your child's college future. This is particularly true on the financial side; however, don't overlook your child's role in making college more affordable. Making the right high school class choices, setting grade goals, and developing good study habits and writing skills can all be worked on, starting in freshman year in high school. Also, thinking seriously about your child's free time and if they are making productive use of it with extracurricular activities is something the more selective colleges focus on. I am a big believer of children identifying a passion or two and making something of it; after all, they should enjoy what they are doing.

What about college-specific activities? If you start focusing on college lists, visits, and SAT/ACT test prep by the fall of high school junior year, you will be fine. Some start earlier, but we say there are enough important things to focus on in high school to keep them busy. As I've said, many families wait until the fall of senior year to begin the laundry list of activities needed to be completed, thus creating a lot of stress at home and potentially missed deadlines.

Because of the many hurdles and lack of information, as well as a lack of clarity on when to begin the process, parents are starting to question whether college is worth it. As a result, some kids are simply not pursuing college, which is a troubling trend.

Summary

Is college worth it? From higher earning potential to better health and a greater contribution to society, the answer is an unequivocal "yes."

The turning point in my education was when I found out about the free financial aid available to me—knowledge is the key to navigating your way through the college system. But getting into the right college can be hard, as there is a lot of competition out there. You need to get yourself noticed, apply early, and do your homework—but the rewards will be great. By the end of this book, you will be fully able to navigate the college planning maze successfully.

In the following chapters, I'll be addressing how to pick the right school, get into your college of choice, pay less for it, and get the help available to you.

3
My Ideal Approach

Did you know there is a right college for every student at an affordable price?

The 40,000-foot view

How can you pay college fees without going broke? The solution is what I call "my ideal approach." Have you ever looked at Google Earth, starting in space before drilling down until you can see your backyard? That's the analogy I'm going to use now, starting with the 40,000-foot view.

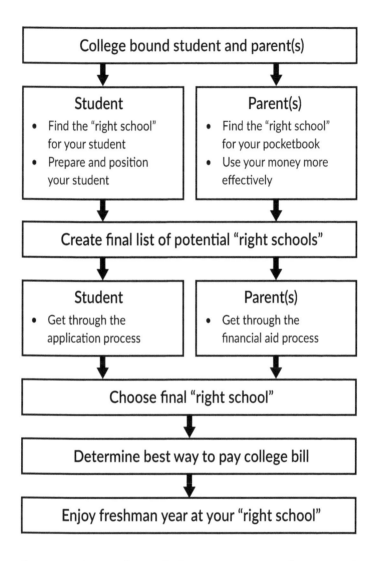

Let me talk you through this. First, start at the top and read through to the bottom, as the steps shown are in chronological order. Second, if I draw a line through the middle of the page, from top to the bottom, the left-hand side is the student's journey, and the right hand side is the parent's journey. Most importantly, you must do all of these steps together in a comprehensive, integrated way to maximize your college success and get the best results. Every step shown is critical. Messing up even one of them will end up potentially costing you lots of money.

If your child goes to the wrong school, it will cost you. How about these statistics? Did you know:

- Only 47% of kids that start at a four-year school get a bachelor's (four-year) degree in four years.[13]

- Only 64% graduate in six years.[14]

- 37% of students transfer at least once in the first six years.[15]

- Only 20% of students starting "the hard way" at a community two-year college received a bachelor's degree within six years.[16]

- Only 34% that started at a two-year college get an associate's (two-year) degree in three years.

---

13 NCES, "Digest of education statistics," Table 326.10 (2021), https://nces.ed.gov/programs/digest/d21/tables/dt21_326.10.asp, accessed 7 September 2023

14 NCES, "Digest of education statistics"

15 P Fain, "More than a third of college students transfer," *Inside Higher Ed (IHE)* (7 July 2015), https://insidehighered.com/quicktakes/2015/07/08/more-third-college-students-transfer, accessed 7 September 2023

16 M Kantrowitz, "Shocking statistics about college graduation rates," *Forbes* (18 November 2021), https://forbes.com/sites/markkantrowitz/2021/11/18/shocking-statistics-about-college-graduation-rates, accessed 7 September 2023

14% transferred somewhere else and 10% are still at the same school in three years.[17]

A big cause of these statistics is students ending up at the wrong school, becoming unhappy, and coming home and/or transferring. If any of this happens, it will cost you even more money than the already steep costs of college over four years. Finding the right school where your child will be happy is critical, but it requires planning and hard work.

Based on my personal experience (public speaking, feedback, and webinar polls), there is a constituency out there that says, "Don't even bother filling out financial aid forms as you will not get any money." However, most of the free money comes from the colleges themselves, not from the government or private scholarships, and the colleges are the gatekeepers of this money—including government free money and loans. To get the free money, you *must* go through the financial aid process and complete those dreaded, confusing financial aid forms.

The 10,000-foot view

To get a better sense of what each of the steps are, and the importance of each, let me present a 10,000-foot view by describing each of the boxes in more detail:

---

17   NCES, "Digest of education statistics"

Students

Find the "right school"

Finding the right college will ensure the student is happy and graduates in four years (not five, six, or more):

- Seek best fit: big, small, country, city.
- Research career paths and choose college majors.
- Efficiently research and visit colleges.

Prepare and position

Make sure the student is attractive to as many schools as possible:

- Create a "brag sheet"; pursue extracurriculars and develop your passions.
- Choose the right high school classes.
- Prepare for and take PSAT/SAT/ACT tests.

Get through the application process

You have to apply to be accepted:

- Complete applications early—do not miss deadlines.

- Prepare for and complete all essays and interviews.

- Submit all supporting materials ("brag sheet," transcripts, recommendations, SAT / ACT test scores).

Parents

Find the "right school" for your pocketbook

Do this by using other people's money rather than your money to pay for college:

- Identify colleges that have money and are willing to give it to you rather than those that don't.

- Match schools with money to your student's interests.

- Create options (don't put all of your eggs in one school's basket).

Use your money in the most effective way

Focus on a comprehensive, integrated college funding plan:

- Pursue *free* money opportunities first—college free money and tax scholarships.

- Identify college-specific financial planning strategies.

Get through the financial aid process

You have to ask for the money to get it:

- Complete all financial aid forms early—do not miss deadlines.

- Submit all supporting materials (tax returns, business supplements, non-custodial forms, etc.).

Determine the best way to pay college bills

Yes, you have to pay before your student can go:

- Understand college payment options (for example, tuition payment plans).

- Research college loan options (only available to college families, not the general public).

- Consider your money options (existing savings / investments, mortgage loans, 401K loans, etc.).

Students and parents

Create a final list of potential "right schools"

- Apply to a minimum of six to eight colleges that will work for all of you (you must have options).

- Create competition among schools for negotiating opportunities.

Choose the final "right school"

This should be a family decision.

- You're admitted. Review all college acceptances.

- Perform final college research and visits.

- Review and compare financial aid packages received—determine the true cost.

- Negotiate with schools of choice for better deal.

As you can see, there is a *lot* of work that needs to be done. Without an integrated step-by-step game plan as to what to work on and when, it increases the odds that critical steps will be missed.

Become informed

We established early on that college is expensive, regardless of which you choose. There are two costs for college: one for the informed and one for the uninformed. You must learn as much as you can, determine and analyze the options, and then make an informed decision about what's best for you and your family. This is probably the second-largest financial decision you will make in your lifetime (the largest being the purchase of your home), so do not take it lightly.

There are lots of myths out there. Most people look at the college sticker price and tell their kids not to bother applying to the more expensive ones. But, of the 82% of students that attend private colleges receiving financial aid, the average discount is 33% (average private school grant of $18,200 divided by the average private school total cost of attendance of $55,800).[18] As a result, the sticker price may mean nothing and many students can attend private schools for the same cost or less than an in-state public college/university.

Further, did you know that there are about 2,300 four-year colleges or universities in the US and that about 67% of them are private with their big scary prices?[19] Keeping the doors open to private schools upfront may increase the odds of finding the right school for both your child and your pocketbook.

Although getting educated about all of the steps in my ideal approach is critical, the biggest piece that is missing is getting the free money from the colleges themselves—the most important but least understood area of opportunity. The lack of information about this still surprises me.

---

18   J Ma and M Pender, "Trends in college pricing and student aid, 2021," (CollegeBoard, 2021), https://research.collegeboard.org/media/pdf/trends-college-pricing-student-aid-2021.pdf, accessed 7 September 2023

19   NCES, "Digest of education statistics," Table 317.10 (2021) https://nces.ed.gov/programs/digest/d21/tables/dt21_317.10.asp, accessed 7 September 2023

Summary

The ideal approach focuses on the "right school" for your student and your pocketbook. You must perform all the recommended steps explained here in a comprehensive, integrated way to maximize college success. It is important to avoid starting at the wrong school, which will cost you extra money and time. For this second-largest financial commitment in your life, you must ignore the myths and be informed, most importantly applying for the free money from the colleges themselves.

In the next section I am going to focus on finding the "right school" for your pocketbook—by getting other people's money vs. your money—with an emphasis on free money from the colleges themselves. In addition, I will show how you get it—by going through what I call the "financial aid process."

PART TWO
FREE MONEY

4

Other People's Money Vs Your Money

Did you know there is FREE money available to help you pay for college?

Common sense example

Let me provide a little more general information before we dive in. First off, what I would like to do is give you what I call a "common sense example" of how there truly is lots of *free* money out there.

Let's say school X, Y, or Z happen to be private schools in your state with big, scary sticker prices. Living on campus ranges from $55K to $80K+ per year. How many people do you know that can write a check for that kind of money? Most people I meet say "very few."

However, these schools all fill up every year. How is that possible? Imagine I am the chief financial officer (CFO) at an expensive college. I have to pay all the bills—the salaries of professors, admin, and staff, plus for the fancy new wok station in the college food hall. The worst thing that could happen is I have an empty seat; therefore, I am willing to give what I call a "tuition discount" (*free* financial aid money) to motivate students to attend the school.

When I worked on Wall Street, one of my managing directors had a screensaver on his computer screen that scrolled with the message: "Revenue is good." Remember, college is a business and getting *some* revenue from a student's family is preferable to no revenue at all. Keep that in mind as we continue our journey.

Let me show you an example of the missed opportunities that a typical family concerned about college costs may make.

Typical family college plan for those concerned about funds

These scenarios assume the parents have discussed the situation with their student and it is a family approach. Many times (such as in my personal story), this is not discussed and the student assumes the family's budget may be close to zero, or even zero (another reason I wrote this book).

OTHER PEOPLE'S MONEY VS YOUR MONEY

Assume your budget is $0–10K per year (all a family think they can afford and/or the student assumes that's the case). That family's student will never pursue options; either not going to college or trying to "go the hard way" (living at home and commuting). Typically, the family looks at four-year college sticker prices to live on campus:

National statistics: annual college costs[20]

Average public IS university	$27,300
Average public OOS university	$44,200
Average private university	$55,800
Elite private university	$80,000+

IS: in-state; OOS: out-of-state. Costs include living on campus with "toothpaste, laundry detergent, and an occasional pizza."

Individual states could have higher prices. Let me repeat the statistics for New Jersey:

Estimated costs for colleges in New Jersey, 2023[21]

IS public	$35,000
OOS public	$55,000
Private	$65,000–80,000+

IS: in-state; OOS: out-of-state. Costs include living on campus with "toothpaste, laundry detergent, and an occasional pizza."

---

20 J Ma and M Pender, "Trends in college pricing and student aid, 2021," CollegeBoard, 2021), https://research.collegeboard.org/media/pdf/trends-college-pricing-student-aid-2021.pdf, accessed 7 September 2023
21 Based on first-hand knowledge of the author

As a result, very quickly, most will determine living on campus is not an option and will not even bother to apply. Privates are ignored, with the assumption there is no way they are affordable. At this point, one of three things happen. They:

1. Apply to in-state public and hope they receive financial aid based on myths (from friends, family, and neighbors)

2. "Go the hard way" (live at home and commute)

3. Do not go to college at all

Did you know that out of 2.7 million US high school graduates in 2021:

- Only 43% enrolled in a four-year college/university.

- Only 19% enrolled in a two-year college.

- Therefore, 38% never enrolled at all.[22]

In the same study in 2010, 32% never enrolled. This, to me, is simply alarming, and the biggest reason for this is lack of information and knowledge about how to make college affordable. Once again, you need to learn about the *free* money.

---

22 National Center for Education Statistics (NCES), "Fast facts: Immediate transition to college," https://nces.ed.gov/fastfacts/display.asp?id=51, accessed 7 September 2023

Finding the solution

What if we can solve the matrix—finding the right schools for the family, no matter what their financial situation or budget is?

Imagine if the following choices were made available to an NJ student by finding the right school, solving the matrix, and getting free money:

- In-state public—on campus: $35K; commute: $20K

- Out-of-state public—on campus: $50K

- Private—$10K

A private school with a sticker price of $80K that you could go to for $10K? How is that possible?

For now, let's assume that no matter what your financial situation is, you can find schools to solve your unique matrix, and pay for colleges you never thought you could afford.

Your unique financial chessboard

If you play chess, you'll know there are rules on how to move the various pieces around the board. For example, the knight has legal moves it can make (two spaces in one direction and one space to the left or right from there). These legal moves are all options; however, the key is: "What is the right move?"

The same is true of your financial chessboard. There are many options (legal moves), but which are the "right moves"? Let's work it out because, let's face it, it is better to use other people's money rather than your own money to pay for your kids' education.

How Will YOU Pay for the High Cost of College?

Other People's Money (Free)	Your Money
Financial Aid	Savings
Family Gifts	Current Income (salaries/Wages)
Education Tax Strategies	Borrow (Loans)

There are insights on everything shown here to become more informed. As we discussed earlier, not everyone will have saved this money. Even if you did, wouldn't you want to save some of your money if you could versus spending on college bills? You could then use the money saved for grad school, for your other kids' future college costs, or your retirement. Besides, as we've discussed, how many of you have free cash flow after paying taxes and your monthly bills? If you plan to borrow, who will you borrow from and how much will you be allowed? If you opt for a loan, are you willing to jeopardize retirement or have less funds available for your other kids?

In summary, there are many insights on how best to free up or create more money. What you need is a comprehensive, integrated college funding plan that considers the following:

- Other people's (*free*) money opportunities first

- Cash flow

- Taxes

- College loan options

- Impact on retirement plans

- Investments

In other words, you need to figure out your own personal and unique financial chessboard.

Other people's money

By now, I'm sure you will agree that the best overall college funding plan is to find and get as much free (other people's) money as possible first, rather than focusing on your own.

Gifts

How many of you have rich relatives to cover the costs of college? Typically, not many; however, if you do, there are strategies to utilize that money for college costs. For example, one of the worst things you can do (if applicable) is have parents/grandparents pay college bills directly. Why? Schools view these "gifts" as "sources" in their financial aid analysis and typically reduce financial aid accordingly. In other words, this family "needs" less financial aid than another family because there is another source of money.

Education tax strategies

There is an overwhelming number of options with the Internal Revenue Service (IRS), which are extremely confusing and complex, but it is useful to understand them. Here are some examples:

- Education tax credits (such as the American Opportunity Tax Credit)

- Savings bonds

- Tuition deductions

- Tax-advantaged 529 plans

- Assets in students' names vs. parents' names

Simply put, as a CPA and financial advisor, there is plenty of information and numerous strategies to learn as part of an overall college plan in these areas alone. However, what I am going to focus on in this book is the best way to make college affordable: financial aid, the best kept secret in America.

Summary

It is important to realize that colleges are businesses and are keen to get *some* money, rather than no money, to pay their bills, so there are opportunities out there to solve the matrix and pay for colleges that you thought were out of your financial league. By learning about your unique financial chessboard, you will recognize the various options to create a comprehensive, integrated college plan, emphasizing finding other people's money first. Along the way, you must learn how to utilize gift money from well-meaning grandparents and to understand the world of IRS options out there before we turn our attention to the big ticket: financial aid, which we will explore in more detail in the next chapter.

5
Financial Aid—The Best Kept Secret In America

Did you know there are tens of billions of dollars in financial aid available every year?

Financial aid

There is about $234.9 billion per year of financial aid available if you know how and where to get it. Of this amount, $175.1 billion is available for undergraduates (meaning attaining a bachelor's degree rather than attending graduate school and pursing a master's degree, PhD, law school, medical school, etc.).[23]

---

23 J Ma and M Pender, "Trends in college pricing and student aid, 2021," (CollegeBoard, 2021), https://research.collegeboard.org/media/pdf/trends-college-pricing-student-aid-2021.pdf, accessed 7 September 2023

Where does financial aid come from?

Let's look at a recent financial aid pie chart that breaks down aid into different categories:

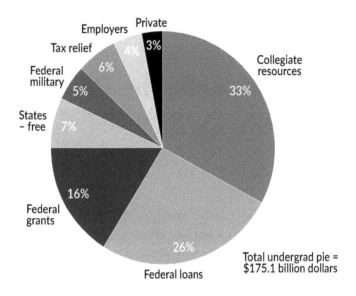

*Trends in **student aid**, 2021*[24]

There is lots of interesting information here, but the two most important takeaways from this chart are:

1. Most free money (not loans) comes from the colleges themselves, not from the government or private scholarships.

---

24 J Ma and M Pender, "Trends in college pricing and student aid, 2021"

2. Colleges are the gatekeepers of 90%+ of finances on this chart. To get access to this money, you must ask for it (by completing financial aid forms).

Other highlights

Federal loans are a large slice of the pie; however, when I talk about financial aid, I focus on the free money that does not have to be paid back, *not* loans. Many schools will mislead you by giving you a loan and calling it financial aid—be wary.

If you are a family of four and make more than $40K per year, you will *not* get any government free money—for example, no Federal Pell Grants.[25] At the time of writing, the maximum Pell Grant per year is about $7,400;[26] however, to get that maximum, the annual family income would typically have to be less than $10K. Let me also point out that private scholarships only make up 1–3% of the total aid pie, which has been consistently true for many years, based on my experience.

Here is some other interesting information from the CollegeBoard "Trends in College Pricing and

---

25 For more information about the Federal Pell Grant, visit https://studentaid.gov/articles/dont-miss-out-on-pell-grants

26 Federal Student Aid, "Federal Pell Grants are usually awarded only to undergraduate students," (2023), https://studentaid.gov/understand-aid/types/grants/pell, accessed 7 September 2023

Student Aid" report from 2021, covering the period 2010/11 through 2020/21:[27]

- College *free* money (collegiate resources) increased by 62%.

- Federal loans decreased by 47%.

- Federal Pell Grants declined by 39%.

Once again, this is further evidence that there may be plenty of free money available from the colleges themselves.

Federal government financial aid

Although we are going to focus on college free money, do not overlook the US federal government financial aid options. Learn what's possible for you:

- Free money is mainly in the form of Pell Grants, typically for families with limited incomes.

- "Work-study" is an on-campus part-time job intended to give you some spending money for "toothpaste, laundry detergent, and an occasional pizza."

- Direct student loans (formerly called Stafford loans) are in the student's name (no cosigner needed), and payments are deferred until the

---

27   J Ma and M Pender, "Trends in college pricing and student aid, 2021"

student ultimately leaves school. Currently, the amount offered is $5,500 maximum for freshman year (plus $6,500 sophomore year, and $7,500 junior and senior years).[28] I generally recommend you consider having the student take these so they have a stake in their own education. I say, "If you still like them when they graduate, you can help them pay them off!"

- The other big loan program is the Parent's PLUS Loan. A parent and/or other adult must get this loan (not the student). The good news is this loan is fairly easy to obtain (you just need an OK credit score for one parent), and you can borrow up to the total sticker price, if desired. These loans would be the last option.

State government financial aid

Similar to the federal government aid, do not overlook your local state financial options and what is possible for you. The following options happen to be where I reside in New Jersey:

- *Free* money:
    - State scholarships (based on merit)
    - Tuition aid grants (based on income/need)

---

28 Federal Student Aid, "The U.S. Department of Education offers low-interest loans to eligible students to help cover the cost of college or career school," https://studentaid.gov/understand-aid/types/loans/subsidized-unsubsidized, accessed 16 October 2023

- – Targeted profession-type scholarships—
  nurses, teachers in minority districts, etc.

- College loans—NJ Class loans. NJ is one of the
  few states that has its own loan program. The
  great news is the NJ Class loan has better rates
  and terms than the Federal Parent PLUS loan.
  This has been true for many years.

- Special 529 tax-advantaged plan. In New Jersey,
  it is called the "NJ Best Plan."

You need to check out the financial aid available in the
state where you live. Every state is different—some
have little; some have lots.

Private scholarships: why chase crumbs?

How about private scholarships? As shown in the
chart above, these represent only 3% of the total
financial aid pie—and between 1–3% has been the
case over my twenty-plus years of college experience.
Rather than private scholarships, I focus on educating
families on how to get the most *free* money from the
colleges themselves.

Some quick points on private scholarships:

- This is a time-allocation question—focus on the
  big money instead (college *free* money).

- Do *not* ignore local scholarship opportunities—
  check out your high school and local clubs
  and associations.

- Be wary of scams.

Are private scholarship services worth it? In general, to get a national scholarship, you need to write an essay explaining why you, versus the thousands of other applicants countrywide, deserve the scholarship. Each scholarship application and/or essay may be different. They involve lots of work—and what are the odds of success?

College and university free money

Colleges have billions of dollars in endowments with no government strings attached. Further, they make a business decision to give back some of that money in the form of financial aid.

Consider the following interesting recent endowment stats for the end of 2020:[29]

- Overall college endowments are at $691 billion.

- The top 120 schools ranked by endowments totaled $515 billion.

---

29 NCES, "Digest of education statistics," Table 333.90 (2022), https://nces.ed.gov/programs/digest/d21/tables/dt21_333.90.asp, accessed 7 September 2023

As per a recent *U.S. News & World Report* article, their top-ranked 397 national universities had an average endowment of about $1.7 billion.[30]

Common myths regarding financial aid

As you can see, there is plenty of money available overall. There are also what I call "myths vs. realities" regarding financial aid. Here are some of the common myths that I hear from families when I speak publicly or via my webinar polls:

- "We make too much money."

- "My kid's grades are too low."

- "Financial aid is limited to 'special' people" (athletes or straight-A students).

- "It's easy to get financial aid."

- "I can figure this out myself."

Typical college financial aid statistics are misleading. For example, what if you heard via a school visit or saw in a college guide something like this: "70% of freshmen at School X receive financial aid and

---

30 S Wood, "10 national universities with the biggest endowments," (13 September 2022), https://usnews.com/education/best-colleges/the-short-list-college/articles/10-universities-with-the-biggest-endowments, accessed 7 September 2023

the average freshman award is $12K"? What would you think?

Many would assume they will get $12K in free money, no matter what. Others would further assume that their kid is above average, so of course they should get more. Unfortunately, that is not how it works, yet these assumptions lead to mistakes.

On the reality side, there is positive news. Colleges need you and are willing to give you discounts. They have empty seats, so are willing to compete with each other and pay for good students. In addition, about 82% of students attending private colleges receive free money and the average free discount is about $20K (remember, this is an average—much more money is available).[31]

Summary

Although there may be some free money from federal and state government grants to private scholarships, I feel is it is most important you focus on pursuing college and university free money. Ignore the myths and misleading statistics and get your applications in. Free money is exactly that—*free*—and it's waiting to be claimed.

---

31   J Ma and M Pender, "Trends in college pricing and student aid, 2021"

Bear in mind that the process is complex and confusing, which can lead to missed opportunities. Therefore, you must find the right school that has free dollars for your unique situation. Even further, you must solve your unique matrix—we will discuss this in more detail later. Next, let's explore financial aid in depth.

6
Need Vs Merit

Did you know that regardless of your financial situation, you can get financial aid?

Types of financial aid

There are two types of financial aid: need-based and non-need-based aid. The vast majority of college guides discuss financial aid in terms of need aid vs. merit aid, and provide misleading statistics accordingly. I do not use the term "merit" on purpose; instead, I use "non-need-based." Why? Well, most people assume merit aid is:

- For straight-A students
- For those that score 1600 on the SAT (or 36 on ACT)

- For top-recruited athletes—for example, a student who can throw a football 60 yards, or score a 10.0 gymnastics routine

They therefore assume, "That's not my kid," and further assume that unless they are living in poverty, they are not going to get any free money. Amazing but true.

As I described earlier, during my many public presentations I often ask the audience whether they think they are going to get any financial aid. The vast majority assume "No," either for the reasons outlined above or because they think they make or have too much money. Yet nothing is further from the truth.

Most people who believe "I am never going to get it" are actually thinking of need-based aid and ignoring non-need-based aid.

Please recognize that:

- No matter what your financial situation, I can show you how to get tens of thousands of dollars per year in *free* money from colleges.

- I can solve any matrix—even if the budget is $0 and your student is at a C-level GPA.

- The only matrix I cannot solve is for a student getting Ds or lower and where the family college budget is $0. I cannot create that miracle.

For hope at this point, please look back at my common sense example outlined in Chapter 4.

Need-based financial aid

No matter what your family financial situation is, you want to first determine *if* you can qualify for need-based aid. You will also need to know your correct annual Student Aid Index (SAI) and see if that will get you free money (most people have no idea). Most importantly, you want to determine the strategies available to reduce your SAI—and make you eligible for need-based aid (vs. not) or make you eligible for even more free need-based dollars. Remember, many people are eligible for more need-based aid than they think.

Conceptual overview of need-based aid

- Financial aid is allocated based on need—your need vs. your neighbor's need countrywide—based on relative income and assets.

- The Department of Education has a need-based analysis formula. It determines an SAI result, which is what you are expected to contribute for your education per year.

- You must complete financial aid forms—for example the FAFSA form (there are more forms than a FAFSA if you want lots of free money);

essentially, you provide your unique income, assets, etc.

- By completing/submitting a financial aid form, an SAI calculator (what I call "the box") produces an SAI as an output. That will determine your eligibility for need-based aid.

- There are lots of myths/misunderstandings regarding need-based aid.

The need-based formula

The Federal Department of Education formula for eligibility for need-based aid[32] is:

Cost of Attendance (COA) – Student
Aid Index (SAI) = "Need."

COA represents the total cost of attendance. Each school annually provides official figures to the Department of Education.

This book focuses on the COA of living on campus, which includes tuition, room, board, books/supplies—everything expected out of your pocket (what I call "the sticker price"). Officially, the school has multiple official COAs—living on campus, off campus (renting an apartment close by), and commuting (living at home).

---

32 Federal Student Aid, "Wondering how the amount of your federal student aid is determined?" https://studentaid.gov/complete-aid-process/how-calculated, accessed 8 September 2023

Schools are typically not transparent about disclosing these total costs on their websites; however, there are third-party vendors that do publish these numbers. Based on my experience, schools that have lots of money typically are more transparent than those that do not give lots of free money. With a little effort, a family can find out what the COA is for a particular school.

SAI represents the Student Aid Index. What you are expected to pay per year is based upon your unique financial situation. This is the mysterious part of the equation that the vast majority of families do not understand.

Remember, this is based on output from an SAI calculator based on data you provide on financial aid forms like the FAFSA. To make it more complicated, there are at least two SAI methodologies / formulas (or boxes): the Federal SAI Methodology and the Institutional SAI Methodology.

The Federal SAI Methodology

In summary, the Federal SAI Methodology:

- Is used by the vast majority of public schools to determine eligibility for giving out their own school's need-based aid (limited money available)

- Is used by some private institutions to determine eligibility for their school's need-based aid

(if they do *not* use the Institutional Methodology described below)

- Is used to disburse federal and state government financial aid funds and loans (if eligible)

- Does *not* assess home equity

- Uses the FAFSA form to collect information

The Institutional SAI Methodology

The Institutional SAI Methodology, in summary:

- Is used by most private universities

- Is used to distribute university funds (*lots* of free money) with no government strings attached

- *Does* assess home equity

- Uses the CSS Profile form to collect information

Free Application for Federal Student Aid

Unfortunately, the vast majority of the public only hear about the FAFSA form and focus all their time and attention on completing that, if at all. Hopefully after reading this book, you will not make that mistake.

In summary, the FAFSA form either:

- Determines eligibility for extremely limited federal and/or state *free* money (for example, limited Federal Pell Grants only if you make less than $40K/year with a family of four)

- Provides access to federal loans that your student has to pay back (maximum of $5,500 freshman year)

Please be aware that many private schools have their own forms and their own formulas besides the two noted above. If you are interested in the tens of thousands of dollars in free money, completing all of those forms is well worth it.

In Chapter 11, I go into more detail about the financial aid process and the forms. For now, let's get a better understanding of how this works (and learning the opportunities).

Understanding need

Let's assume your SAI is $30K, based on your unique income, assets, etc. on your financial aid forms. Take a look at the following illustration:

Financial need

	College A (public)	College B (private)
COA	$30K	$80K
Minus SAI	$30K	$30K
Equals need	$0	$50K

This hypothetical example is for illustration purposes only. Actual results may vary.

College A: $30K – SAI of $30K = need of $0... what does that mean?

It means:

- You would not be eligible for any need-based aid at College A.

- But you would be eligible for non-need-based aid—more on that later.

College B: $80K – SAI of $30K = need of $50K... what does that mean?

- You would be eligible for $50K of need-based aid at College B.

- Let's also assume College B's financial aid policy is if you have need at College B and are accepted at College B, you are guaranteed essentially $50K in *free* money.

Comparing the results of College A vs. College B

Let me introduce my concept of "true cost": Sticker price (COA) – expected free money = true cost:

- True cost at College A: $30K COA / sticker price – $0 expected free money = $30K true cost.

- True cost at College B: $80K COA / sticker price – $50K expected free money = $30K true cost—guaranteed. (Even if your student is the last one admitted to the school or the last one before the waiting list.)

It would cost the same to attend College A as College B! Let's digest this for a moment and assume the following:

- College A is an in-state public school with an all-in live-on-campus cost of $30K.

- You do not get non-need-based aid at College A (remember, you are not eligible for need-based aid).

- The family budget is OK with a cost of $30K per year; therefore, your expectation is $30K per year at College A.

This means that if you previously thought you couldn't look at schools with big, scary sticker prices, now, based on this new "true cost" insight, you can rethink the whole situation.

If your budget was limited to $30K (and not much more), here's what you would want to do to solve your unique matrix:

- Assume there are limited College As in the state in which you live.

- Include as many viable College As as possible (they cannot charge more than the sticker price).

- Find as many viable College Bs as possible—
  there are lots of College Bs.

- Increase the odds that you will find college
  success because now you can look at many
  more schools you did not think you could
  afford vs. limiting your choices to only College
  As (i.e., many more "right" college options for
  your student).

Some of you may be saying, "I cannot afford the in-state public school College A price, so what about me?" Stay tuned—remember, no matter what your financial situation is, I can show you how to get tens of thousands of dollars in *free* money.

Also, now that you know your SAI, you are guaranteed the funds you are "eligible for," right? No. Not all schools are College Bs—more on that later.

What you want to know next

The next major step regarding need-based financial aid is finding the right schools that will give you the most free money based on need. Which schools will give you the best shot at getting more free money?

- Some schools give more money than others.

- Some schools meet 100% of *need* (College Bs).

- Others don't.

If you are focusing on need-based aid, wouldn't you want those schools that give the most need-based aid? Ideally, schools that meet your need 100% with essentially all free money?

Self-help

One thing that particularly frustrates me is that many schools consider loans or an on-campus job "financial aid." Not me. I consider the *free* money (gift aid) that does not have to be paid back financial aid.

- Many schools meet need with *free* money:
    - Gift aid—free money that does *not* have to be paid back
    - Grants/scholarships
- Too many schools meet need with self-help money:
    - On-campus jobs (you have to earn money)
    - Loans (you have to pay back money)

I call loans or a job self-help—the loans have to be paid back, and you have to earn money if you work. Some schools meet need with free money; others don't. Wouldn't you want to know this before you apply?

Public vs. private schools

Choose your college wisely, as some schools have more money than others:

- As a general rule, private schools have more money than public schools.

- Many students can attend a private school for the same cost or less than an in-state public school.

The great news is that roughly 75% of colleges and universities in the US are private, increasing the odds of finding the right school for your student. Further, do you remember from earlier that 82% of students attending private schools receive financial aid and the average free money is $18,200, or an average 33% off the sticker price?

Understanding schools' aid policy

The next challenge is to figure out what the financial aid policy is for each school. Public statistics can be misleading and information is not readily available. Further, you must be wary of college website net price calculators (NPCs)—see Chapter 13 for more details.

If you heard, "51% of students receive financial aid, and the average free money is $12K," what would you think? In summary:

- Assume the statistics are "correct," but looking at the disclosure above, what if most of the free money went to football players at the school? Even though the statistics would be right, there will be little money in financial aid for regular (non-football-playing) students; therefore, not much to students based on academics or even "need."

- Contrast that to College B, for example.

If applicable, wouldn't you want to know that?

Finding the right financial schools for you and your pocketbook

No matter what your unique situation is, imagine a list of right financial schools for you. Assume there is a database that says, based on your financial situation, "Here is a list of ranked schools that will give you the most, more, average, less, and least *free* money, depending on your SAI."

Assuming your SAI is $0–15K, which would be the right schools for your pocketbook? Take a look at this table:

SAI: $0-15K

	Category	Sticker price	"True cost"
Most "free money"	Private 100% NB (All)	$55–85K+	$0–15K
	Top 5%:		
	Public IS	$25–35K	$0–15K
	Public OOS	$40–55K	$0–15K
	Private TD	$55–85K+	$0–15K
	Private < 100% NB	$55–85K+	$0–15K

(Continued)

SAI: $0–15K (cont.)

	Category	Sticker price	"True cost"
	Public IS (< 96%)	$25–35K	$25–35K
Least "free money"	Public OOS (< 96%)	$40–55K	$40–55K
	Private TD (< 25%)	$55–85K+	$55–85K+
	Private < 100% NB (< 25%)	$55–85K+	$55–85K+

This hypothetical example is for illustration purposes only. Actual results may vary.

This is a snapshot of a database sorting where you could expect the most to the least free money for an estimated SAI of $0–15K. (Please note that I did not include "more", "average", or "less" options—only "most" and "least".) To further explain this table:

- **Sticker $:** Cost of attendance living on campus at that particular type of school

- **True cost $:** Net cost after receiving expected *free* money at that particular type of school

- **Public IS:** Public in-state college/university

- **Public OOS:** Public out-of-state college/university

- **Private TD:** Private school that gives tuition discounts (non-need-based aid)

- **Private 100% NB:** Private school that gives 100% need-based aid (College B)

- % = where in the freshman applicant pool (so, "<25%" means in the bottom 25%)

If we condense the table for this SAI, it looks like this:

SAI: $0-15K

	Category	Sticker price	"True cost"
Most "free money"	Private 100% NB (All)	$55-85K+	$0-15K
Least "free money"	Public IS (< 96%)	$25-35K	$25-35K
	Public OOS (< 96%)	$40-55K	$40-55K
	Private TD (< 25%)	$55-85K+	$55-85K+
	Private < 100% NB (< 25%)	$55-85K+	$55-85K+

This hypothetical example is for illustration purposes only. Actual results may vary.

In summary, College Bs—schools that have a financial aid policy that would meet your need 100% with essentially all *free* money—would be your best choice. "All" means even if the last one accepted ("one before the waiting list"), you are guaranteed the *free* money; in other words, your student just has to get accepted.

In this case, if the College B school had a sticker price of $80K and your SAI was $10K, you will essentially get $70K in free money and go to that school for $10K—guaranteed. Remember my common sense example from Chapter 4? Now you can see how a student with an SAI of $0–10K can actually go to a four-year school and live on campus for $10K or less based on their SAI—simply find the right school.

If you were not in the top 5% (<96%) of the applicant pool at a public school, you would not expect to receive any free money and would be stuck at the sticker price—let's say $35K. This is also true at an out-of-state public school, but with much higher sticker prices.

Assuming both schools were equally attractive to your student, would you rather pay $10K or $35K? Whichever you ultimately choose, wouldn't it be nice to have those options?

Some of you may say, "I make too much money and will never be eligible for need-based aid" (and therefore never get financial aid). Remember what I have said previously, no matter what your financial situation is, I can show you how to get tens of thousands of dollars in *free* money.

Non-need-based financial aid

If you can never get need-based financial aid, let me explain non-need-based financial aid. Essentially, this means finding schools that will give you what I call "tuition discounts."

How to access non-need-based aid:

- Getting tuition discounts from private schools with lots of money

- Positioning your student for merit aid—what I call "the top 5%" of that school's freshmen entering class

There is an opportunity for families who make too much money to qualify for need-based financial aid to get *free* money from schools too.

Understanding non-need-based financial aid

The vast majority of college publications, college financial aid statistics, and the colleges themselves break down financial aid into two categories:

1. Need-based aid

2. Merit aid

When you hear the term "merit," what do you think? Most people probably think, "That money is not for my student." Why? For most people "merit" means a "top" academic student with straight As or a talented athlete that will get an athletic scholarship. As a result, many conclude that they will not be eligible for merit aid, and further, they believe they will never get any need-based aid either. In my experience, this is one of the most misunderstood areas of financial aid and leads to lots of missed opportunities. That's why I call this area of opportunity "non-need-based" aid instead of "merit."

Think of my common sense example from Chapter 4 and remember that college is a big business—someone figured out a long time ago that if I can build a college for C-level high school students, I can make lots of money!

Just like the need-based section, let's find the right financial schools for your pocketbook. Assuming your SAI is $80K+, imagine a list of right financial schools for you, even if you will never get need-based aid.

Look at the table below; for this situation, there is a different priority list of most to least free money:

SAI: $80K+

	Category	Sticker price	"True cost"
Most "free money"	Top 5%:		
	Public IS	$25–35K	$0–15K
	Public OOS	$40–55K	$0–15K
	Private TD	$55–85K+	$0–15K
Least "free money"	Public IS (< 96%)	$25–35K	$25–35K
	Public OOS (< 96%)	$40–55K	$40–55K
	Private 100% NB (all)	$55–85K+	$55–85K+
	Private < 100% NB (All)	$55–85K+	$55–85K+
	Private TD (<25%)	$55-85K+	$55-85K+

This hypothetical example is for illustration purposes only. Actual results may vary.

This table is a snapshot of a database sorting where you could expect the most to the least free money for an estimated SAI of $80K (never eligible for need-based aid). (Please note that I did not include "more", "average", or "less" options—only "most" and "least".) See the key on page 68 for an explanation of the terms used here.

By condensing the table for this situation, it looks like this:

SAI: $80K+

	Category	Sticker price	"True cost"
Most "free money"	Private TD (top 5%)	$55–85K+	$0–15K
	Private TD (50–95%)	$55–85K+	$35–50K
Least "free money"	Public IS (< 96%)	$25–35K	$25–35K
	Public OOS (< 96%)	$40–55K	$40–55K
	Private 100% NB (all)	$55–85K+	$55–85K+

This hypothetical example is for illustration purposes only. Actual results may vary.

If you can find schools that have made a business decision to give tuition discounts to attract students, regardless of a family's financial situation, these would be the best options to save yourself tens of thousands of dollars. (Please note that even if your child is not "top 5%" at a TD school, you can still get substantial free money. Shown here is a student who is in the top 50% of the applicants—50-95%—and they may get tens of thousands of dollars. Whereas, at a public school, they would probably get zero free dollars unless in the top 5%).

If you have a top student (straight As, 1500+ SAT), your friends, family, and/or neighbors may tell you no matter where your student goes, "Of course you should get scholarships." What if this were not true? It all depends on whether you have found the right school financially. If you happen to find a school that gives you plenty of tuition discounts *plus* has lots of money, it could be true. In fact, if you pick the right private school, you may get close to a full scholarship.

What if the school selected was a College B—what I call "a 100% need-based school"? Unfortunately, the vast majority of those types of schools do not give any merit-based aid; instead, they only give out need-based aid, if eligible. As a result, in this family's case, they would get $0 free money and be stuck at sticker price.

How crazy is that? Let me show you that this is not just crazy; it is also completely arbitrary, and it explains why so many people miss out.

Comparing elite private schools with dramatically different results

Imagine your college-bound student is interested in going to college in Washington, D.C. with a view to a career in the State Department, the CIA or the Supreme Court. Further, you find out two of the top schools in D.C. are Elite Private School 1 and Elite Private School 2, and you decide to do college visits. Let's assume the sticker prices at both schools is $80K and your college budget is $35K/year—essentially the cost of an in-state public school where you live. Let's also assume your SAI is greater than $80K, even after any financial strategies.

As part of the official visits, the financial aid director at Elite Private School 1 says something like: "70% of freshmen get financial aid, and the average *free* money is $45K per year." Assume, Elite Private School 2 says essentially the same thing, and for both schools these statistics are true.

Given this information, you tell your student, "If you get the average $45K in *free* money from either elite private school, we will let you attend." This would be because the true cost to attend either would be $35K and equal to your public school budget. Because of this understanding, you encourage your student to apply and see what happens.

Arbitrarily, your student applies only to Elite Private School 1, not Elite Private School 2. In case you are not aware, applying to these two elite private schools— and most private schools—is a much more complex application process than applying to a typical public school. It involves writing essays, doing interviews, and more.

Meanwhile, you learn that to be considered for financial aid overall, parents need to ask for it. This means you have to complete and submit financial aid forms (more than the FAFSA) to Elite Private School 1, and you do so. (Remember, colleges are the gatekeepers for distributing most financial aid.)

Your student figures out all of the complex application requirements, does all the extra work, and gets accepted (receiving a letter from the admissions office). Congratulations!

Now you wait for a financial aid letter from Elite Private School 1, which comes separately from the financial aid department. You receive the award letter and find out your student is awarded zero dollars in *free* money. You contact the financial aid office and say, "We attended a college visit, and your director said the average *free* money award was $45K. Our student is above average, so we expected more than $45K—there must be a mistake."

The financial aid office rep reviews your family's file and eventually informs you, "Your SAI is greater than our cost of attendance, and Elite Private School 1 only gives need-based aid—no merit money—so, unfortunately, you are not eligible for any *free* money here." (It is what I call, a College B.) As a result, you are stuck with the sticker price.

Because of this, you determine you cannot or do not want to spend the $80K+ to send your student to Elite Private School 1. Even though this was the student's top choice, you send them to the less expensive public school instead. But what if you had been better informed and understood that finding the right school financially upfront would have changed the result?

Elite Private School 2 competes with Elite Private School 1 for top applicants; however, they have a different financial aid policy. Elite Private School 2 also gives what I call "tuition discounts" (merit aid) and has lots of money. They made a business decision to attract top applicants that would not be eligible for need-based aid and are unwilling to pay full sticker prices. Elite Private School 2 is generous with meeting need, if eligible, but do not guarantee to meet everyone's need 100%. Simply put, this means they would give more need-based aid to those higher up the applicant pool and may give zero need-based aid to someone near the bottom.

As a result, if your family had learned about Elite Private School 2's financial aid policy, and your student saw this as a top choice school, similar to Elite Private School 1, applying to Elite Private School 2 would have been the better option. If your student was a top applicant, they may have gotten close to a full scholarship. Even if they were in the middle of the accepted applicant pool, they probably would have gotten the average $45K in *free* money. As a result, you would be willing to send your student to D.C. ($80K COA − $45K *free* money = $35K true cost). All you needed to do was find the right school for your pocketbook. Isn't that amazing?

What if your family's situation was different? Let's assume your family's SAI is $30K and you have an annual budget of $30K. Additionally, your student is in the bottom 25% of the freshman applicant pool at both D.C. schools. Let's also assume you do the same college visits and hear the same information, but your student arbitrarily applies to Elite Private School 2, *not* Elite Private School 1.

Great news—your student is accepted at Elite Private School 2, but the *free* money offered is only $10K. As a result, your family is unwilling to spend the $70K at this school ($80K COA − $10K free), and your student went to the less expensive public school.

If your family had learned about Elite Private School 1's financial aid policy, and if your student had been accepted, they would have been guaranteed the $50K in *free* money and gone to that school for $30K. How crazy and arbitrary is that?

Avoid surprises

You do *not* want to be surprised. Therefore, a critical component of getting *free* money is understanding each school's financial aid policy:

- Know the school's financial aid policy *before* you apply.

- Make sure school choice is matched to your unique goals and college budget.

- Be wary of school statistics.

- Learn what your actual SAI is, and find out if, with strategies, you could reduce this to a level that allows you to get free need-based aid.

- If ultimately eligible for need-based aid, target schools that give lots of need-based aid—ideally 100% need-based schools.

- Remember what I said before—no matter what your financial situation is, I can show you how to get tens of thousands in *free* money from the colleges themselves. Therefore, if you are never able to get need-based aid, target schools that give tuition discounts and have lots of money.

FAFSA simplification

At the time of writing, the Department of Education was proposing sweeping new changes to the FAFSA form and the related Federal Methodology SAI calculation, which they are calling "FAFSA Simplification." These are the biggest changes I have seen in my more than twenty years of experience—these changes are not "simplification"; instead, they will result in major confusion and further complexities, if and when implemented (they are scheduled for December 2023, and will affect students applying for financial aid beginning Fall 2024).

Some of these changes include:

- Replacing the "Expected Family Contribution" (EFC) with a new term: the "Student Aid Index" (SAI)

- Changing the formula for calculating the SAI (vs. the EFC), including getting rid of the "more than one student in school" family benefit, plus assessing more business assets that were previously excluded from the Federal Methodology

My analysis of the "new" proposed FAFSA

I do not see much "simplification" at all and sincerely wonder how such a term was settled upon. For example, the new SAI-calculated output will determine eligibility for need-based financial aid, just like the old "EFC" number did. In other words, eligibility for financial aid will still be: *cost of attendance – SAI = eligibility for need-based aid*. Why change the name?

Further, in my analysis of the changes to the calculated SAI, the new number appears that it will be *higher* "apples to apples" than the previously calculated EFC for many families; therefore, making some *less* eligible for need-based aid. For example:

- Assume your family's EFC was $30K. If you had twins attending college, your federal EFC was split in two: one child had half ($15K) and the other had the other half ($15K). Therefore, if your two students attended a school that costs $30K, each child would be eligible for $15K in need-based aid.

- With the new SAI calculation, the "multiple child in school" benefit is scheduled to be eliminated. As a result, each student would now have a $30K SAI; therefore, neither one is eligible for need-based aid at a $30K school.

Another major change regards treatment of businesses in the Federal Methodology. Previously, if you had a business with fewer than 100 employees, no business information was entered on the FAFSA form. Now it appears business information will be asked for in many more situations than before.

The most amazing thing to me about these new changes is that they only affect the FAFSA and the Federal Methodology—*not* the Institutional Methodology or the CSS Profile. As of the time of writing, there have been no indications of that methodology or the form changing by CollegeBoard (who is the vendor for this form/methodology), or how it will impact the financial aid eligibility of schools that require the CSS Profile. Remember, the private schools (with lots of *free* money) that require the CSS Profile are determining eligibility for need-based aid using their process/form, with no government strings attached. Beginning as early as December 2023, we may need both an SAI and an EFC. How is this going to simplify anything for families planning on college?

To make things even worse, in recent years the FAFSA form has been made available to the public on 1 October for new high school seniors and their families. As of now, the Department of Education has already announced the new FAFSA will be delayed until December 2023. Assuming that the proposed deadline is met, plus there are no major launch issues, that will create even more confusion than in a "normal" year.

Please double-check what the current situation is, get informed, and plan accordingly. Despite all of this, the fundamental idea of finding the most *free* money from your right schools (solving *your* matrix) as presented in this book does *not* change.

Summary

Financial aid is available to everyone and there are two types available: need-based and non-need-based aid. To determine if you can qualify for need-based aid, you need to know your correct SAI and, importantly, to determine the strategies available to reduce this to be eligible for the most free dollars.

Choose your schools wisely, as some have more money than others, and do your research to make sure you understand their policies before you apply. If you are not eligible for need-based aid, non-need-based financial aid is what you focus on, which involves finding schools that will offer "tuition discounts." Remember, regardless of your financial situation, there is free college money available. With the right preparation, you can find the financial aid that will secure a place in the right school for your child.

Now that you have a much better idea of how financial aid works, plus you realize that most free money comes from the colleges themselves, how do you find the right schools for your unique situation? Let's explore that question now.

PART THREE
FINDING YOUR FREE MONEY

7
Right School Vs Wrong School

Did you know that choosing the right school will give your kid better odds of college success?

Choosing the right college

How do you choose the right college? Besides finding one you can afford, what about picking one that your student likes—one where they will be happy? If you don't, you may end up paying college bills for five or six years to get a four-year degree.

Remember, I previously said that *all* the ideal approach steps must be done in a comprehensive, integrated way to maximize success. If you mess up one of them, it could affect your whole plan.

So, did your student pick the right school (the best fit for them so they are happy)? Will your student finish:

- …where they started?
- …in four years?
- …at all?

If not, it will cost you.

As we mentioned in Chapter 3, bear in mind:

- Only 47% of kids that start at a four-year school get a bachelor's (four-year) degree in four years. Only 64% graduate in six years.[33]
- 37% of students transfer at least once in the first six years.[34]
- Only 20% of students starting "the hard way" at a community two-year college received a bachelor's degree within six years.[35]

---

33 NCES, "Digest of education statistics," Table 326.10 (2021), https://nces.ed.gov/programs/digest/d21/tables/dt21_326.10.asp, accessed 7 September 2023

34 P Fain, "More than a third of college students transfer," *Inside Higher Ed (IHE)* (7 July 7 2015), https://insidehighered.com/quicktakes/2015/07/08/more-third-college-students-transfer, accessed 7 September 2023

35 M Kantrowitz, "Shocking statistics about college graduation rates," *Forbes* (18 November 2021), https://forbes.com/sites/markkantrowitz/2021/11/18/shocking-statistics-about-college-graduation-rates, accessed 7 September 2023

- Only 34% that started at a two-year college get an associate's (two-year) degree in three years. 14% transfer somewhere else and 10% are still at the same school in three years.[36]

Think about your community—how many times have you seen kids go off to school and then return back home a few weeks later? The schools know this and overbook the dorms (like an airline). How many times do you hear that kids are supposed to be in doubles (dorm rooms) but start in triples? For my niece's freshman year dorm room (at a top private New England university), she started in the student lounge!

Think about this. A kid gets to the school and immediately starts calling home. The typical response from a parent will be, "Oh, come on, toughen it out for a while and you should be fine." A few days later, the child is still miserable, and now the parent knows this may be a problem. They say, "Hmm, let me check out the school's refund policy," and they discover that if the student comes home within two to three weeks of the start of the school semester, they can get a refund. If the student stays longer, the refund is $0. Therefore, many kids come home.

How does this happen? The student picks the wrong school.

---

36   NCES, "Digest of education statistics"

Reasons for choosing the wrong school

The biggest reason for choosing the wrong school is that the student does not think about the campus environment and just assumes they will be fine wherever they go. Other valid reasons include:

- **Friends:** How many students pick a school because their best friend or significant other is going there? What are the odds of that working out over time?

- **Final Four:** How many students pick a brand-name school? Think of the NCAA Final Four basketball tournament. It amazes me, but the year after the last tournament, applications for the schools that make the Final Four spike up the following year.

- **Start late/miss deadlines:** Many students do not realize that college applications and all related activity must be completed by the beginning of their senior year in high school. If they wait until then to start the process, it results in lots of stress and missed opportunities.

- **Ineffective visits:** Many students start at a college without ever visiting it. What are the odds of finding the best fit this way?

- **Sticker price:** The vast majority limit their choices based on sticker price.

- **The easy way out:** Many students, if left on their own, will work only on the easiest applications and will avoid schools that ask for more work (such as essays and interviews).

How to find the right school

To find the best fit and your greatest chance of success, think about the following:

- **Have a purpose:** If college is for you, start early. Set high school goals and focus on making the right decisions. For example, set grade goals, pick the right classes, choose what you do with your free time (jobs, sports, community service) wisely, and standardize test strategies.

- **Self-discovery assessments:** Learn what's unique about you and your future aspirations. Think about career options—which college majors or courses do you need to get there?

- **Effective college visits:** Have a plan. We always recommend visiting local schools, if possible, to simply get a feel of big vs. small, country vs. city before you travel long distances to see schools.

- **The best fit:** Ultimately, what is the right school, unique to you? Once you identify the best fit, create other potential best-fit options.

Ultimately, it all comes down to the best fit, unique to your child. Think about these rhetorical questions:

"Will my student be equally happy at a large school and a small school? A school in the city and a school in the country?"

Effective college visits

Although this book is intended to focus on finding free money, I want to add a little more about college visits—the best way to figure out the best fit for your student.

The official campus visit

First, I recommend the family do one "official" campus visit by fall of the high school junior year. This official visit comes in two parts:

1. An information session

2. A college tour

The information session is typically in an auditorium with PowerPoint presentations, coffee, and donuts. This is worthwhile because you can get a lot of information about why you should apply to their school rather than others.

Then you will go on the college tour, which is usually led by actual students. These sessions are normally done regularly; just check the colleges' websites and be sure that appointments are not necessary. On these tours, you should ask any candid questions you want answers to. If you are concerned about drugs, crime, dorm conditions, etc. you can gain some real insights. The key is that the school does not want to mislead you and have you come to campus to be unhappy (and complain or leave the school), so they coach the guides to answer these questions directly and honestly. The school wants you to be happy because it affects their statistics.

All you want to accomplish is for your child to walk around the campus and to (hopefully) think, "Hey, in two years, this will be me. Maybe I should start thinking about it!"

The college fair

Second, I suggest you attend a "college fair," again by fall of the high school junior year. Typically, your local high school will host multiple colleges to come and set up tables and invite a representative. Students or families can walk around, gather information, and ask questions to a variety of schools. The college fair will force the students to realize all the choices available to them and allow them to get their minds working toward understanding that a lot of work and research is going to be needed to pick the right school.

What I hope will happen for your student, as they are walking out with bags and bags of "stuff," is to say, "Wow, there are so many great college choices, how am I going to pick one?"

If the above two things happen, "mission accomplished."

Visiting further schools

Next, we want to visit more schools. My philosophy is to make the college visit process as efficient and rewarding as possible. The key is to try and identify what the "right" school is for your student. That will ensure that they are happy and will graduate on time rather than being unhappy, transferring, and graduating in five, six, or seven years.

Big, small, country, city

Initially, narrow the fit using "big, small, country, city" as an initial guideline. The most efficient way to start is to think local—there is no need to create a preliminary college list and travel around the country to visit schools. Instead, find schools within the local area and visit a big city school, a small city school, a big country school, and a small country school. In this way, you effectively allow the student to see and get a feel for each type of school.

Imagine you are located in central New Jersey. You could start by visiting Rutgers University (a big public university in a city), The College of New Jersey (a smaller community-based public school in the suburbs), and Monmouth University (a smaller private school in the suburbs). This allows you to get a sense of a large public school, a smaller public school, and a smaller private school, as well as a feel for a more urban school against a more suburban school. You could expand your horizon a little further and visit schools in and around New York City (NYU, Columbia, or Fordham) or Philadelphia (Drexel, University of Pennsylvania, Temple, or St. Joseph's) to get an idea of different "feels" and gain an understanding of what a big city school may feel like. Another type of school we recommend is a smaller private school "in a college town." For this, we recommend Eastern Pennsylvania (Lehigh, Bucknell, or Lafayette, for example). You can do any of these trips in a day and see a variety of schools.

When should these visits be done?

We are big fans of letting kids be kids and allowing them to enjoy everything high school has to offer. Typically, we would suggest visiting at least one actual campus by the fall of junior year (as described previously). More of these "local" visits can be accomplished leisurely through spring of junior year. Some of you may not be able to wait and you may enjoy visiting colleges earlier as part of a family vacation far away from home. This is fine—if you enjoy doing these visits, please go ahead.

If possible, visit the colleges when classes are in session. You will get a much better feel of the campus that way, rather than when the campus is empty. The key is efficiency. Get a feel for the big, small, country, and city dynamic and have fun with it.

Common mistakes

Imagine all the mistakes people make throughout this process. Think about all the marketing materials you are going to receive at your home and all the leaflets and information you will be picking up here and there. The colleges will all try to connect with you, but out of 2,300 or so colleges and universities across this country, what are the odds of you opening a brochure for the "right school" for your student? If something catches your eye, that is fine, but otherwise try and ignore these mailings, because all schools look perfect on glossy paper.

Driving and/or flying around the country to visit a list of schools is inefficient and largely unproductive, especially early in the process. There is a much better and more efficient process to follow (see above) that will succeed in providing superior results. (However, I do want to acknowledge that if you live in a rural state, "local" visits may not be practical; my general recommendation still applies – start with "practical" local.)

College is one of the costliest decisions families make in their lifetimes—in fact, it is second only to buying a family home—but most people do not spend the time to truly get educated and understand their options. If your family becomes one of those statistics that it takes more than four years to get a four-year degree, it is going to cost you.

Your student should create options. Applying to only one or two schools is a risky strategy. What if they are not accepted? We recommend you come up with a minimum of six to eight best-fit alternatives and apply to all of those schools. In addition, create a competitive mix to increase your odds of acceptance, for example, three to four targets, one to two reach schools, and one to two likelies (what many call "safeties").

However, what I describe above is a minimum "rule of thumb." There are some situations that require applying to a minimum of many more schools. For example, what if your family goal is to go to one of the eight Ivy League schools, plus you learn your SAI is $10K, and all you need to happen is your talented student needs to get accepted at one of these schools and you are guaranteed $70K+ of free money if accepted? As a result, you may need twelve to fourteen minimum schools to make sure your student gets into one of many College Bs.

Summary

Not every college is right for every kid, but finding the right one gives them a head start while minimizing costs. There are many reasons for choosing the wrong schools, but having a purpose through high school, thinking about career options, and effectively visiting a range of colleges—using big, small, country, city as a guideline—will prepare you to find the best fit for your student. What's not to like?

Now that you have some idea of the right schools for your student and how this should not be overlooked in the ideal approach, the next chapter is dedicated to finding the right school for your pocketbook.

8
The Right School For Your Pocketbook

Did you know some schools provide more financial aid than others?

So, your child has done their part and found the right schools for them—great job! If money is a factor, however, it's important to note that even if your student does all of the above and applies to a nice mix of right schools, it does not mean you can afford them.

This is one of my biggest general criticisms of our high school guidance departments. Many high schools provide resources to help students research and select colleges to apply to, but they generally do a terrible job in helping people figure out how to pay for them.

Scattergrams

One of the things that frustrates me is that high schools put together what I call "scattergrams" of college admissions. It would be a much more valuable tool to create a scattergram of where high school kids actually go. This would allow communities to focus on getting students into four-year colleges they could afford versus "going the hard way," or worse still, not going at all. Remember the college enrollment statistics I described in Chapter 4?

Have you seen a scattergram of college applications/acceptances from your local high school? What it typically shows is, for a given class year, where the kids applied and what the results were. Also typically included is the students' GPA and test scores. Scattergrams can be a useful tool to show kids and parents how they may fare by applying to a particular school relative to other students from that high school.

Let me give you an example:

	Weighted GPA	GPA	SAT	Result
Elite college 1				
Student 1	5.0	4.0	1580	Accepted
Student 2	4.8	3.9	1550	Accepted
Student 3	4.5	3.7	1500	Waitlisted
Student 4	4.2	3.5	1400	Declined
Student 5	3.9	3.3	1300	Declined

	Weighted GPA	GPA	SAT	Result
Student 6	3.8	3.1	1200	Declined
Very competitive college 2				
Student 3	4.5	3.7	1500	Accepted
Student 5	3.9	3.3	1300	Accepted
Student 6	3.8	3.1	1200	Waitlisted
Student 7	3.8	3.1	1200	Declined
Student 8	3.7	3.0	1100	Declined
Competitive college 3				
Student 4	4.2	3.5	1400	Accepted
Student 7	3.8	3.1	1200	Accepted
Student 8	3.7	3.0	1100	Waitlisted
Student 9	3.5	2.9	1050	Declined
Student 10	3.4	2.8	1000	Declined

This hypothetical example is for illustration purposes only. Actual results may vary.

Although these scattergrams show where kids were accepted (or waitlisted or rejected), what they do not show is where each student actually ended up.

What happens if a student is accepted at ten schools but never goes to one because they can't afford it? They may "go the hard way," if the schools are close by and, if so, what are their odds of success? Not good, based on the college graduation success statistics I shared in Chapter 3. Even potentially worse, what if the schools are not close to home? In that case, they may try to start by going to a local two-year community college, or not go at all.

As a community, wouldn't it be better to have kids in four-year schools that they could afford; ideally also in the right schools to maximize college success?

Some typical family scenarios

Let me give you an idea of what typically happens to most families' college decisions depending on individual family budgets. In addition, I am going to show you how to "solve the matrix" by finding schools they never thought they could afford, regardless of the family budget. Remember what I said earlier, "I can show each of you how to get thousands, even tens of thousands of free money from colleges no matter what your financial situation."

1. $10K budget/year

Remember in Chapter 4 I presented a scenario to show you how a typical family that does not think they can pay more than $10K per year may miss opportunities? As a reminder, let me present it again here:

Assume the budget is $0–10K per year (all the family think they can afford and/or the student assumes that's the case). That family's student will never pursue options; therefore, the student will either not go to college at all or may try to "go the hard way," i.e., live at home and commute.

Here is an overview of what typically happens:

- The family looks at four-year college sticker prices to live on campus.

- Cost of attendance/sticker price (living on campus):
    - In-state public—on campus: $35K; commute: $20K
    - Out-of-state public—on campus: $50K
    - Private—$80K

Quickly, most will determine living on campus is not an option and will not even bother to apply, and private colleges will be ignored due to the assumption there is no way they are affordable. At this point, one of three things happen. They:

1. Apply to an in-state public school and hope they receive financial aid, based on myths (from friends, family, and neighbors)

2. "Go the hard way" (live at home and commute)

3. Do not go to college at all

However, what if the following choices were made available by finding the right school, solving the matrix, and getting free money?

- In-state public—on campus: $35K; commute: $20K

- Out-of-state public—on campus: $50K

- Private—$10K

Now that you are more fully informed, let's assume that the family who thought they could not pay more than $10K per year for college had an SAI of $10K. In this case, the matrix solution would be what I call a "College B"—a school that meets 100% of need. If the school costs $80K, and the student was accepted, the family would end up paying only $10K/year, guaranteed. Imagine that.

2. $20K budget/year

Overly simplified, a family budget of a maximum of $20K per year will give you the following sticker-price options:

- In-state public—on campus: $35K; commute: $20K

- Out-of-state public—on campus: $50K

- Private—$80K

The vast majority of people are going to focus on price, so if the family determines the most they will spend is $20K, the college plan will most likely be to live at home and commute. If the budget is even less, they may commute to a two-year community college or not go at all. This will dramatically reduce the chances of college success.

What if the following choices were made available by finding the right school, solving the matrix, and getting *free* money:

- In-state public—on campus: $35K; commute: $20K

- Out-of-state public—on campus: $50K

- Private—$20K

Remember, 67% of the schools in this country are private with scary sticker prices, but that is where you get the money. Wouldn't you want to learn about those schools for your student rather than limiting them to one or two choices close to home and hoping they are happy?

If the family's SAI was $20K or less, once again finding 100% need-based schools would be the best option.

What if the family's SAI is $35K per year, or more, but the preferred budget is still $20K? The solution would be schools that are willing to give tuition discounts. The family would not be able to go to a 100% need-based school (College B) unless they were willing to pay close to their SAI ($35K).

3. $35K budget/year

Let's use the same assumptions as the second family scenario, but in this case the family is OK with an in-state tuition—say a budget of $35K/year—but not willing to pay anything more. Overly simplified, here are the following sticker-price options:

- In-state public—on campus: $35K

- Out-of-state public—on campus: $50K

- Private—$80K

Essentially, once their research is done, this typical family will limit choices to in-state public and:

- Avoid/eliminate private schools with big, scary sticker prices

- Try to get out-of-state publics on list (with relative sticker prices less than privates) and hope that the parents let them escape from them (get further away from home)

Again, this means *huge* missed options for a vast majority of families. Why not seek options? What if the following choices were made available by finding the right school, solving the matrix, and getting *free* money?

- In-state public—on campus: $35K

- Out-of-state public—on campus: $50K

- Private—$35K

Assuming this was true, wouldn't you want to know about those schools/options? If the family's SAI was $35K or less, once again finding 100% need-based schools would be the best option. If the family's SAI is greater than $35K, look for schools that also offer tuition discounts.

4. $50K budget/year

Let's assume the family budget is $50K per year. Overly simplified, you have the following sticker-price options:

- In-state public—on campus: $35K

- Out-of-state public—on campus: $50K

- Private—$80K

In this case, essentially all public schools in-state would be options, plus most of the out-of-state schools in the country would be in reach. Once again, the family may not pursue the private schools that they do not think they can afford.

This is a *huge* missed option for a vast majority of families. What if the following choices were made available by finding the right school, solving the matrix, and getting *free* money:

- In-state public—on campus: $35K

- Out-of-state public—on campus: $50K

- Private—$50K

Assuming this were true, wouldn't you want to know about those schools/options? If the family's SAI was $50K or less, once again, finding 100% need-based schools would be the best option. If the family's SAI is greater than $50K, look for schools that also offer tuition discounts. This would open up the odds of finding the right school for your student, rather than limiting them to public school options.

5. $80K+ budget/year

Lastly, what if you are OK with spending $80K+ per year and your family's SAI was over $80K? Wouldn't you be interested if you could save money at schools just like your student's top choice (where you do not expect any *free* money to be available)? This could mean saving money for grad school, law school, or medical school; for other siblings going to college later; or, if not, preserving your money for your own retirement.

Finding schools that will save you tens of thousands of dollars per year may be worth checking out. Do you remember my scenario presented in Chapter 6 regarding Washington, D.C.? In that case, two elite universities arbitrarily had different financial aid policies. For this type of family, finding the ones that offered significant tuition discounts would be preferable to those that only give need-based aid.

Summary

Whatever your budget—whether it is $10K, $20K, $35K, $50K, or $80K+ per year—you have options. The key is to "solve the matrix," no matter what your college budget. Sticker price means nothing—what matters is true cost after financial aid.

At this point, I hope you are beginning to feel more confident that there may be real options for schools you never thought you could afford. In the next chapter, I provide more details on how to solve *your* unique matrix. I also outline specific recommendations of types of right schools for nine different family scenarios, providing even more detailed analysis and options, including schools to avoid.

9
Nine Matrix Solutions

Did you know that the true cost of college depends on your unique financial situation?

Solving your matrix

Everyone is unique. The biggest key to getting *free* money from colleges is finding the right schools, ideally right for your student as well as for your pocketbook. I call it "solving your matrix."

Remember the ideal approach described in Chapter 3? Here is the chart I presented earlier:

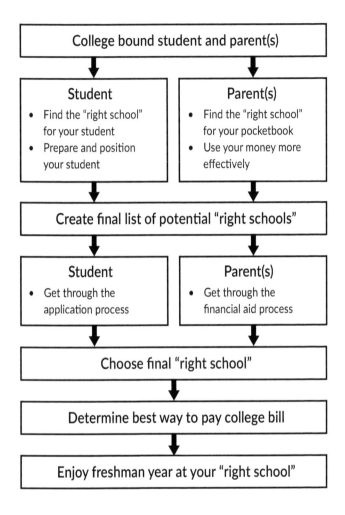

I also introduced the concept "solve your matrix" in the last chapter, too. Let me explain this concept more fully here. To create a final list of potential right schools, you must solve your unique matrix. The solution is different for each family's or student's situation. Based on inputs, there is a particular list of right schools for both the student and the parent.

Students' unique inputs
(the right school for your student)

- Grades

- Test scores

- College major

- Best-fit campus environment—big, small, country, city

Parents' unique inputs
(the right school for your pocketbook)

- College budget

- Family financial situation—need-based vs. non-need-based

Imagine, based on these inputs, there is a unique list of college choices for your student and your family; once again, assuming no matter what your financial situation is, this matrix can be solved.

Matrix solutions—an overview

Let's assume that by now you have a good idea of the right schools vs. the wrong schools for your college-bound student (i.e., "big, small, country, city…"). I am now going to provide you with quick recommendations for right schools *financially* for nine family situations: three different types of students (A, B, and C) with three varying financial situations (low, middle, and high income). This is intended to give you a reference of the recommended right school solutions unique to most types of families.

1. Top (A) student

Let's assume a straight-A student: unweighted GPA close to 4.0, SAT 1500+ or ACT 34/35+.

Scenario 1: Low-income family

The family has a low income (<$100K) and low SAI (<$15K). (This was my situation way back in high school.)

Recommendation: Target 100% need-based schools. If accepted, the student is guaranteed to get *free* money to reduce their cost close to their SAI. For example, School 1 (100%) has a sticker price of $80K and if SAI is $10K, they will provide $70K in *free* money per year.

Scenario 2: Middle-income family

The family has a middle income ($100–150K), middle SAI ($25–30K), and is OK with a budget of $25–35K/year.

Recommendation: Target 100% need-based schools. If accepted, the student is guaranteed to get *free* money to reduce their cost close to their SAI. For example, School 1 (100%) has a sticker price of $80K and if SAI is $30K, they will provide $50K in *free* money per year.

Scenario 3: High-income family

The family has a high income ($250K+), high SAI ($80K+), and a budget of $35–40K/year (or are willing to spend lots more, but would prefer to save money).

Recommendation: Target private tuition discount schools with lots of money. If the student is in the top 5% of freshmen entering class, they may qualify for merit awards, potentially up to a full scholarship. If they are at least in the top 50%, the student may still be eligible for tens of thousands of dollars in merit awards. For example, School 2 (private TD) has a sticker price of $80K and the school provides $40K in *free* money per year.

2. Above-average (B) student

Let's assume an above-average (B) student: unweighted GPA close to 3.0, SAT 1200–1300.

Scenario 1: Low-income family

The family has a low income (<$100K) and low SAI (<$15K).

Recommendation: Target 100% need-based schools. If accepted, the student is guaranteed to get *free* money to reduce their cost close to their SAI. For example, School 1 (100%) has a sticker price of $80K and if SAI is $10K, they will provide $70K in *free* money per year. (Remember, even if the student is the last admitted, they are still guaranteed the *free* money.)

Scenario 2: Middle-income family

The family has a middle income ($100–150K), middle SAI ($25–30K), and is OK with a budget of $25–35K/ year.

Recommendation: Target 100% need-based schools. If accepted, the student is guaranteed to get *free* money to reduce their cost close to their SAI. For example, School 1 (100%) has a sticker price of $80K and if SAI is $30K, they will provide $50K in *free* money per year.

Scenario 3: High-income family

The family has a high income ($250K+), high SAI ($80K+), and a budget of $35–40K/year (or are willing to spend lots more, but would prefer to save money).

Recommendation: Target private tuition discount schools with lots of money. If the student is in the top 5% of freshmen entering class, they may qualify for merit awards, potentially up to a full scholarship. If they are at least in the top 50%, the student may still be eligible for tens of thousands of dollars in merit awards. For example, School 3 (private TD) has a sticker price of $80K and the school provides $40K in *free* money per year.

3. Average (C) student

Let's assume an average (C) student: unweighted GPA close to 2.0, SAT 1000–1100.

Scenario 1: Low-income family

The family has a low income (<$100K) and low SAI (<$15K).

Recommendation: Target 100% need-based schools. If accepted, the student is guaranteed to get *free* money to reduce their cost close to their SAI. For example, School 1 (100%) has a sticker price of $80K and if SAI is $10K, they will provide $70K in *free* money per year. (Remember, even if the student is the last admitted, they are still guaranteed the *free* money.)

Scenario 2: Middle-income family

The family has a middle income ($100–150K), middle SAI ($25–30K), and is OK with a budget of $25–35K/ year.

Recommendation: Target 100% need-based schools. If accepted, the student is guaranteed to get *free* money to reduce their cost close to their SAI. For example, School 1 (100%) has a sticker price of $80K and if SAI is $30K, they will provide $50K in *free* money per year.

Scenario 3: High-income family

The family has a high income ($250K+), high SAI ($80K+), and a budget of $35–40K / year (or are willing to spend lots more, but would prefer to save money).

Recommendation: Target private tuition discount schools with lots of money. *If* the student is in the top 5% of freshmen entering class, they may qualify for merit awards, potentially up to a full scholarship. If they are at least in the top 50%, the student may still be eligible for tens of thousands of dollars in merit awards. For example, School 4 (private TD) has a sticker price of $80K and the school provides $40K in *free* money per year.

Matrix solutions—in detail

I will now go into the analysis in much more detail. Besides where to get the most *free* money, I will outline other practical options plus highlight the worst option(s) (schools to avoid) for each scenario.

Please note, there are infinitely more scenarios that are unique to each family situation. For example, "What if I am a middle-income family but I am *not* OK with spending $25–35K per year?" Or, "What if my child is an A-/B+ student?"

Clearly, we cannot cover every possible scenario in a book like this, but this more detailed section should provide a greater roadmap of how to analyze your situation, no matter what your unique circumstances may be. Here goes.

1. Top (A) student

Let's assume a straight-A student: unweighted GPA close to 4.0, SAT 1500+ or ACT 34/35+.

Scenario 1: Low-income family

The family has a low income (<$100K), low SAI (<$15K), and their budget is <$15K/year.

Recommendation: Target 100% need-based schools. If accepted, the student is guaranteed to get *free* money to reduce their cost close to their SAI. For example, School 1 (100%) has a sticker price of $80K and if SAI is $10K, they will provide $70K in *free* money per year.

Other options

- Private tuition discount schools with lots of money. If the student is in the top 5% of freshmen entering class, they may qualify for merit awards, potentially up to a full scholarship. If they are at least in the top 20–30%, the student may still be eligible for tens of thousands of dollars in merit awards that may get them to their target budget.

- In-state public schools. If the student is in the top 5% of freshmen entering class, they may qualify for merit awards, potentially up to a full scholarship.

- Out-of-state public schools. If the student is in the top 5% of freshmen entering class, they may qualify for merit awards, potentially up to a full scholarship.

Schools to avoid

- Public schools (both in-state and out-of-state), if the student is *not* in the top 5% of freshmen entering class. There will most likely be little or no free money, and the family will be stuck close to sticker price.

- Private tuition discount schools that do *not* have lots of money. Although some free money may be available, it will typically not be substantial.

- Private tuition discount schools with lots of money, if the student is *not* in the top 20–30% of freshmen entering class. Although some free money may be available, it will typically not be substantial enough to get the student to their target budget.

Scenario 2: Middle-income family

The family has a middle income ($100–150K), middle SAI ($25–30K), and is OK with a budget of $25–35K/year.

Recommendation: Target 100% need-based schools. If accepted, the student is guaranteed to get *free* money to reduce their cost close to their SAI. For example, Washington, D.C. School 1 (100% need-based) has a sticker price of $80K and if SAI is $30K, they will provide $50K in *free* money per year.

Other options

- Private tuition discount schools with lots of money. If the student is in the top 5% of freshmen entering class, they may qualify for merit awards, potentially up to a full scholarship. If they are at least in the top 50%, the student may still be eligible for tens of thousands of dollars in merit awards.

- In-state public schools. These cannot charge students more than sticker price. Plus, if the student is in the top 5% of freshmen entering class, they may qualify for merit awards, potentially up to a full scholarship.

- Out-of-state public schools. If the student is in the top 5% of freshmen entering class, they may qualify for merit awards, potentially up to a full scholarship.

Schools to avoid

- Public schools (out-of-state), if the student is not in the top 5% of freshmen entering class. There will most likely be no free money, and the family will be stuck close to sticker price.

- Private tuition discount schools that do *not* have lots of money. Although some free money may be available, it will typically not be substantial.

- Private tuition discount schools with lots of money, if the student is *not* in the top 50% of freshmen entering class. Although some free money may be available, it will typically not be substantial enough to get the student to their target budget.

Scenario 3: High-income family

The family has a high income ($250K+), high SAI ($80K+), and a budget of $35–40K/year (or are willing to spend lots more, but would prefer to save money).

Recommendation: Target private tuition discount schools with lots of money. If the student is in the top 5% of freshmen entering class, they may qualify for merit awards, potentially up to a full scholarship. If they are at least in the top 50%, the student may still be eligible for tens of thousands of dollars in merit awards. For example, Washington, D.C. School 2 (private TD) has a sticker price of $80K and the school provides $40K in *free* money per year.

Other options

- In-state public schools. These cannot charge students more than sticker price. Plus, if the student is in the top 5% of freshmen entering class, they may qualify for merit awards, potentially up to a full scholarship.

- Out-of-state public schools. Some may have sticker prices in the $40K range. For those with sticker prices of $50K+, if the student is in the top 5% of freshmen entering class, they may qualify for merit awards for tens of thousands of dollars, potentially up to a full scholarship.

Schools to avoid

- Out-of-state public schools (sticker prices of $50K+), if the student is *not* in the top 5% of freshmen entering class. There will most likely be little or no free money, and the family will be stuck close to sticker price.

- Private tuition discount schools that do *not* have lots of money. Although some free money may be available, it will typically not be substantial enough to get the student to their target budget.

- Private tuition discount schools with lots of money, if the student is *not* in the top 50% of freshmen entering class. Although some free money may be available, it will typically not be substantial enough to get the student to their target budget.

2. Above-average (B) student

Let's assume an above-average (B) student: unweighted GPA close to 3.0, SAT 1200–1300.

Scenario 1: Low-income family

The family has a low income (<$100K), low SAI (<$15K), and their budget is <$15K/year.

Recommendation: Target 100% need-based schools. If accepted, the student is guaranteed to get *free* money to reduce their cost close to their SAI. For example, Washington, D.C. School 1 (100% need-based) has a sticker price of $80K and if SAI is $10K, they will provide $70K in *free* money per year. (Remember, even if the student is the last admitted, they are still guaranteed the *free* money.)

Other options

- Private tuition discount schools with lots of money. If the student is in the top 5% of freshmen entering class, they may qualify for merit awards, potentially up to a full scholarship. If they are at least in the top 20–30%, the student may be still eligible for tens of thousands of dollars in merit awards that may get them to their target budget.

- In-state public schools. If the student is in the top 5% of freshmen entering class, they may qualify for merit awards, potentially up to a full scholarship.

- Out-of-state public schools. If the student is in the top 5% of freshmen entering class, they may qualify for merit awards, potentially up to a full scholarship.

Schools to avoid

- Public schools (both in-state and out-of-state), if the student is *not* in the top 5% of freshmen entering class. There will most likely be no free money, and the family will be stuck close to sticker price.

- Private tuition discount schools that do *not* have lots of money. Although some free money may be available, it will typically not be substantial.

- Private tuition discount schools with lots of money, if the student is *not* in the top 20–30% of freshmen entering class. Although some free money may be available, it will typically not be substantial enough to get them to their target budget.

Scenario 2: Middle-income family

The family has a middle income ($100–150K), middle SAI ($25–30K), and is OK with a budget of $25–35K/ year.

Recommendation: Target 100% need-based schools. If accepted, the student is guaranteed to get *free* money to reduce their cost close to their SAI. For example, Washington, D.C. School 1 (100%) has a sticker price of $80K and if SAI is $30K, they will provide $50K in *free* money per year.

Other options

- Private tuition discount schools with lots of money. *If* the student is in the top 5% of freshmen entering class, they may qualify for merit awards, potentially up to a full scholarship. If they are at least in the top 50%, the student may still be eligible for tens of thousands of dollars in merit awards.

- In-state public schools. These cannot charge students more than the sticker price. Plus, if the student is in the top 5% of freshmen entering class, they may qualify for merit awards, potentially up to a full scholarship.

- Out-of-state public schools. Some may have sticker prices in the $40K range. For those with sticker prices of $50K+, if the student is in the top 5% of freshmen entering class, they may qualify for merit awards for tens of thousands of dollars, potentially up to a full scholarship.

Schools to avoid

- Out-of-state public schools (sticker prices $50K+), if the student is *not* in the top 5% of freshmen entering class. There will most likely be little or no free money, and the family will be stuck close to sticker price.

- Private tuition discount schools that do *not* have lots of money. Although some free money may be available, it will typically not be substantial enough to get the student to their target budget.

- Private tuition discount schools with lots of money, if the student is *not* in the top 50% of freshmen entering class. Although some free money may be available, it will typically not be substantial enough to get the student to their target budget.

Scenario 3: High-income family

The family has a high income ($250K+), high SAI ($80K+), and a budget of $35–40K/year (or are willing to spend lots more, but would prefer to save money).

Recommendation: Target private tuition discount schools with lots of money. If the student is in the top 5% of freshmen entering class, they may qualify for merit awards, potentially up to a full scholarship. If they are at least in the top 50%, the student may still be eligible for tens of thousands of dollars in merit awards. For example, Washington, D.C. School 2 (private TD) has a sticker price of $80K and the school provides $40K in *free* money per year.

Other options

- In-state public schools. These cannot charge students more than the sticker price. Plus, if the student is in the top 5% of freshmen entering class, they may qualify for merit awards, potentially up to a full scholarship.

- Out-of-state public schools. Some may have sticker prices in the $40K range. For those with sticker prices of $50K+, if the student is in the top 5% of freshmen entering class, they may qualify for merit awards for tens of thousands of dollars, potentially up to a full scholarship.

Schools to avoid

- Out-of-state public schools (with sticker prices of $50K+), if the student is *not* in the top 5% of freshmen entering class. There will most likely be little or no free money, and the family will be stuck close to sticker price.

- Private tuition discount schools that do *not* have lots of money. Although some free money may be available, it will typically not be substantial enough to get the student to their target budget.

- Private tuition discount schools with lots of money, if the student is *not* in the top 50% of freshmen entering class. Although some free money may be available, it will typically not be substantial enough to get the student to their target budget.

3. Average (C) student

Let's assume an average (C) student: unweighted GPA close to 2.0, SAT 1000–1100.

Scenario 1: Low-income family

The family has a low income (<$100K) and low SAI (<$15K).

Recommendation: Target 100% need-based schools. If accepted, the student is guaranteed to get *free* money to reduce their cost close to their SAI. For example,

Washington, D.C. School 1 (100% need-based) has a sticker price of $80K and if SAI is $10K, they will provide $70K in *free* money per year. (Remember, even if the student is the last admitted, they are still guaranteed the *free* money.)

Other options

- Private tuition discount schools with lots of money. If the student is in the top 5% of freshmen entering class, they may qualify for merit awards, potentially up to a full scholarship. If they are at least in the top 20–30%, the student may still be eligible for tens of thousands of dollars in merit awards that may get them to their target budget.

- In-state public schools. If the student is in the top 5% of freshmen entering class, they may qualify for merit awards, potentially up to a full scholarship.

- Out-of-state public schools. If the student is in the top 5% of freshmen entering class, they may qualify for merit awards, potentially up to a full scholarship.

Schools to avoid

- Public schools (both in-state and out-of-state), if the student is *not* in the top 5% of freshmen entering class. There will most likely be little or no free money, and the family will be stuck close to sticker price.

- Private tuition discount schools that do *not* have lots of money. Although some free money may be available, it will typically not be substantial.

- Private tuition discount schools with lots of money, if the student is *not* in the top 20–30% of freshmen entering class. Although some free money may be available, it will typically not be substantial enough to get them to their target budget.

Scenario 2: Middle-income family

The family has a middle income ($100–150K), middle SAI ($25–30K), and is OK with a budget of $25–35K/year.

Recommendation: Target 100% need-based schools. If accepted, the student is guaranteed to get *free* money to reduce their cost close to their SAI. For example, Washington, D.C. School 1 (100% need-based) has a sticker price of $80K and if SAI is $30K, they will provide $50K in *free* money per year.

Other options

- Private tuition discount schools with lots of money. If the student is in the top 5% of freshmen entering class, they may qualify for merit awards,

potentially up to a full scholarship. If they are
at least in the top 50%, the student may still
be eligible for tens of thousands of dollars in
merit awards.

- In-state public schools. These cannot charge
  students more than the sticker price. Plus, if the
  student is in the top 5% of freshmen entering
  class, they may qualify for merit awards,
  potentially up to a full scholarship.

- Out-of-state public schools. Some may have
  sticker prices in the $40K range. For those with
  sticker prices of $50K+, if the student is in the top
  5% of freshmen entering class, they may qualify
  for merit awards for tens of thousands of dollars,
  potentially up to a full scholarship.

Schools to avoid

- Out-of-state public schools (sticker prices of
  $50K+), if the student is *not* in the top 5% of
  freshmen entering class. There will most likely
  be little or no free money, and the family will be
  stuck close to sticker price.

- Private tuition discount schools that do *not* have
  lots of money. Although some free money may
  be available, it will typically not be substantial
  enough to get the student to their target budget.

- Private tuition discount schools with lots of
  money, if the student is *not* in the top 50% of

freshmen entering class. Although some free money may be available, it will typically not be substantial enough to get the student to their target budget.

Scenario 3: High-income family

The family has a high income ($250K+), high SAI ($80K+), and a budget of $35–40K / year (or are willing to spend lots more, but would prefer to save money).

Recommendation: Target private tuition discount schools with lots of money. If the student is in the top 5% of freshmen entering class, they may qualify for merit awards, potentially up to a full scholarship. If they are at least in the top 50%, the student may still be eligible for tens of thousands of dollars in merit awards. For example, Washington, D.C. School 2 (private TD) has a sticker price of $80K and the school provides $40K in *free* money per year.

Other options

- In-state public schools. These cannot charge students more than the sticker price. Plus, if the student is in the top 5% of freshmen entering class, they may qualify for merit awards, potentially up to a full scholarship.

- Out-of-state public schools. Some may have sticker prices in the $40K range. For those with sticker prices of $50K+, if the student is in the top 5% of freshmen entering class, they may qualify for merit awards for tens of thousands of dollars, potentially up to a full scholarship.

Schools to avoid

- Out-of-state public schools (sticker prices of $50K+), if the student is *not* in the top 5% of freshmen entering class. There will most likely be little or no free money, and the family will be stuck close to sticker price.

- Private tuition discount schools that do *not* have lots of money. Although some free money may be available, it will typically not be substantial enough to get the student to their target budget.

- Private tuition discount schools with lots of money, if the student is *not* in the top 50% of freshmen entering class. Although some free money may be available, it will typically not be substantial enough to the student to their target budget.

The true cost

As you can see, most *free* money comes from private schools, not public schools. Opening the doors to private schools you never thought you could afford creates many more options.

Remember, about 67% of the four-year colleges and universities in the USA are private with high sticker prices; however, what matters is the true cost after receiving any free financial aid.

Summary

The key to reducing your college costs is solving your unique matrix. The solution is unique to each family's or student's situation. This chapter demonstrates this with quick recommendations for right schools *financially* for nine family situations: three different types of students (A, B, and C) with three varying financial situations (low, middle, and high income). It goes to prove there is a right school for every family, no matter your budget and it is worth pursuing private schools, as this is where the most *free* money comes from.

PART FOUR

DISCOVERING MORE FREE MONEY

10
Reduce Your SAI

Did you know there are a number of options to reduce your SAI?

More opportunities

As previously stated, no matter what your financial situation, there are ways to find schools that will give you tens of thousands of *free* money per year. Each and every one of you should find out your SAI to help you figure out which schools to target. If need-based, focus on those schools.

That certainly makes a lot of sense, but what if you could get even *more* free money? This chapter is all about focusing on two huge opportunities that most people miss:

1. If you are eligible for need-based aid, let me show you how you can get more.

2. If you are not eligible for need-based aid, let me show you how you can become eligible. This will enable you to explore many more school choices.

Most people never learn about these possibilities and miss out. But not you.

In Chapter 6 we discussed the concept of need-based aid in some detail, including what an SAI is and how it works. One of the things I showed you is that if a school's costs are more than your SAI, you are then eligible for free need-based financial aid.

Remember this?

Financial need

	College A (public)	College B (private)
COA	$30K	$80K
Minus SAI	$30K	$30K
Equals need	$0	$50K

This hypothetical example is for illustration purposes only. Actual results may vary.

What if you could get even more free money? Who wouldn't want that? Let me show you how to reduce your SAI and be eligible for more free money. Remember, mistakes happen—even at College Bs—and you can fix errors, plus negotiate better deals; something we will explore in Chapter 12.

Financial aid "loopholes"

Like any game, if you do not learn the rules, you will probably lose. Let's learn how we can win. There are what I call "financial aid loopholes" that, with proper planning, enable you to reduce your SAI. Why not find out what is possible for your family?

- It is perfectly legal and ethical to make use of rules to save money, for example, tax loopholes. Most people know that having home mortgage debt may be tax deductible vs. credit card debt.

- Knowing more, gets you *more* free money.

Understanding this opportunity

Let's assume a family of four makes $80K per year, plus has a net worth (assume net assets) of close to $870K. The following chart shows a typical family with this income and asset profile. Bear in mind each individual family situation is unique (number of family members, deductions/credits, etc.). Let's look at this chart and point out some highlights:

Financial aid legal "loopholes"—reduce SAI?

	Institutional	Federal
Initial SAI	$32,800	$32,000
After Strategy 1	$31,400	$32,000
After Strategy 2	$24,325	$32,000
After Strategy 3	$18,575	$23,950
After Strategy 4	$8,900	$12,300

Strategies referenced are hypothetical and for illustration purposes only. Actual results may vary.

- Many people may think this family (assuming no mistakes are made on the financial aid forms—a huge assumption) will not get any financial aid.

- However, their initial SAI is actually about $32K, as per two different formulas. Let's round this to $30K SAI to better understand the key points.

- Let's imagine that through planning ahead of time and implementing the four strategies outlined above, the family's SAI could be reduced to about $10K (rounding off $8,900 and $12,300). What does this mean?

Let's take a look at College A vs. College B now, *after* strategies.

Financial need (after strategies)

	College A (public)	College B (private)
COA	$30K	$80K
Minus SAI	$10K	$10K
Equals need	$20K	$70K

This hypothetical example is for illustration purposes only. Actual results may vary.

By reducing SAI, this family would be eligible for even *more* free money:

- Their SAI has been reduced from about $30K to $10K.

- Previously, they were not eligible for need-based aid at College A (their need was $0). Now their need is $20K. Therefore, they would now be eligible for $20K in *free* money, whereas previously they would be eligible for $0.

- More importantly, at College B their SAI is reduced from $30K to $10K, making their need $70K, not $50K. They are now guaranteed to get $70K in *free* money at as many College Bs as they can find. (Remember, I described College B as a school that will meet your need with 100% *free* money.)

SAI reduction strategy example

Before I go any further, many people ask: "What are the strategies to reduce my SAI?" There are way too many to go through here, but let me give you one example I typically present to an audience when I publicly speak.

Let's assume I have two families that have each saved $40K to be spent on college costs for their child. They each put this money into an investment account in the parents' name. So I can make the math easier to follow, they each have a great financial advisor who is getting a 10% return as ordinary income on their tax returns. Uncle Sam will tax those earnings, so, $40K multiplied by 10% equals $4K that flows through the tax returns. Let's assume they are in a 25% marginal tax bracket, $1K ($4K in ordinary income multiplied by 25%) is collected by the IRS in taxes.

Let's assume that one family (Family A) meets a financial or tax advisor (or reads about this strategy somewhere) who suggests that if you switch the $40K into an account that's in the student's name (what is known as a custodial account, commonly titled as either an "UGMA" or an "UTMA" account), you could save the $1K you pay in taxes every year. Family A does that, and they are happy to get the extra $1K per year in tax savings.

On the other hand, Family B never learns of this strategy, and therefore keeps the account in the parents' name.

We'll fast forward to filling out financial aid forms time. To keep it simple, let's assume the SAI formula assesses a 25% SAI charge on any assets in the student's name, and 5% on any assets in the parents' name. The theory is that any assets in the student's name will be spent for college costs vs. those in the parents' name, which may have to be used for ongoing family living expenses or to protect the parents' future retirement plans. Make sense?

For Family A, the $40K college account will add $10K to their SAI calculation ($40K multiplied by 25%), whereas the SAI charge for Family B is only $2K ($40K multiplied by 5%). Does that seem fair?

Further, let's assume both families intend to use the $40K for college bills; the exact same plan. Simply because one account is in the student's name and one is in the parents' name, there is a difference of $8K in the SAI calculation. Do you like your financial/tax advisor now?

If you don't think it's fair, then one strategy for Family A would be to move the money back into the parents' name before submitting the financial aid forms. This would result in an $8K SAI reduction.

At this point, I'm going to flag up a warning. This is not meant to be investment or financial advice, so please do not go and implement this strategy without consulting with a competent college planner, financial advisor, and/or CPA. Making moves on "your financial chessboard" requires getting the right guidance and advice.

However, the purpose of this example is to show you that, with proper planning, there are opportunities to look less rich and potentially reduce your SAI.

Many of you may say, "That's not me, I make $150K, not $85K, so that won't work for me." Let's review the next chart, assuming the family makes $150K per year with $730K in net worth/net assets:

Financial aid legal "loopholes"—reduce SAI?

	Institutional	Federal
Initial SAI	$72,800	$49,500
After Strategy 1	$54,800	$49,500
After Strategy 2	$45,500	$49,500
After Strategy 3	$32,300	$36,750
After Strategy 4	$26,900	$30,600

This hypothetical example is for illustration purposes only. Actual results may vary.

Assuming initial SAIs are $50–73K, imagine if they could be reduced to about $30K (I am rounding off the $26,000 and $30,600 figures in the chart).

Keeping it simple:

- Clearly, they could look at College As with the assumption they are OK with a bill of $30–35K/year.

- But now they could look at all College Bs and go guaranteed for close to $30K/year, even with an annual income of $150K/year.

What if a family makes $300K and thinks, "That's not me." Remember, prior to the proposed "FAFSA simplification" changes, financial need was determined by the Expected Family Contribution (EFC) versus the term SAI. Think about this: the "F" in EFC referred to "family" contribution, not a "student", so if you had two from one family in college at the same time, each child had a piece of the total EFC; therefore, each family's EFC would be split up between the two students. Based upon the prior chart, when two children were in school at the same time, each child's EFC was about half of the total.

Even if your income was $300K, with two in school at the same time, after strategies, each student's EFC was $25–30K. What does that mean?

- At College Bs you were guaranteed the *free* money.

- If one student went to College B, and one student went full-time to a community college, the student's EFC at College B was still $25–30K.

Think about that huge potential opportunity, if applicable. Hopefully, now you can see it's well worth checking out what your actual EFC is and whether there are opportunities to reduce it before completing your financial aid forms.

At the time of writing, the Department of Education was proposing to eliminate this "two in school at the same time" EFC family reduction as part of

"FAFSA simplification". It is unclear whether the private schools and their institutional formulas will also change. Make sure you double-check the current rules if you have this unique situation. (For more information regarding FAFSA simplification, please see the end of Chapter 6).

Summary

No matter what your financial situation, you may want to find out your SAI—before and after strategies—and see what is possible. Most people never do this, so make sure you don't miss out. Explore opportunities such as financial aid "loopholes" and SAI reduction strategies to lower your SAI. Doing so could make you eligible for even *more* free money.

11
Ask First...

Did you know every school has a different financial aid process?

Going through the process

To access this *free* college money, you must ask for it. That means completing those financial aid forms, like the FAFSA, CSS Profile, institutional forms, verification, and more. Remember, colleges are the gatekeepers of 90%+ of all the financial aid awarded each year, therefore, to get this money you must go through the financial aid process.

In summary, this process includes the following major general steps:

1. Apply.

2. Get an offer—only an estimate.

3. Analyze the award.

4. Negotiate.

5. Finalize the award—verification and tax information.

6. Make the college decision.

7. Accept the award.

Unfortunately, each school's process is unique, making this process even more complicated. So, how do you apply for aid?

Free Application for Federal Student Aid (FAFSA)

All schools require the FAFSA if you want the financial aid office involved. This must be completed for all schools if you are interested in government aid and loans. Remember, in general, public schools meet need with government money or loans, not their own money.

Go to studentaid.gov to see the form, which has many pages/boxes to complete.

What is amazing to me is that because of the financial aid myths I described earlier in Chapter 5, only 52%

of the 2022 senior class completed the FAFSA form (meaning 48% did not).[37] Do *not* let that be you.

CSS Profile

Most private schools with significant free money require the CSS Profile (that's where most free money comes from). To gain access to the CSS Profile, you must register for it first.

The CSS Profile includes many more questions than the FAFSA. Here are some major differences:

- CSS Profile asks for three years' income information; FAFSA asks for one.

- CSS Profile asks about home equity; FAFSA does not.

- CSS Profile asks about all businesses; FAFSA doesn't ask for business info on all businesses, only some.

- CSS Profile includes supplemental school questions, including information on retirement plans, who owns cars, etc.; FAFSA does not.

- CSS Profile asks about non-custodial parents (ex-spouses); FAFSA does not.

---

37 Bill DeBaun, "Class of 2022 FAFSA completions rebound, climb 4.6% year-over-year," (National College Attainment Network, 9 July 2022), www.ncan.org/news/610844/Class-of-2022-FAFSA-Completions-Rebound-Climb-4.6-Year-Over-Year.htm, accessed 16 October

Why? Because they can. Fundamentally, the CSS Profile must be consistent with FAFSA; otherwise, a school has the right to ask for more details or explanations. You'll want to avoid red flags.

School institutional forms

Many private schools (as you have discovered, the ones with the money) require you to complete even *more* forms. One example is what we call the "institutional form." This is the school's own form, in addition to the FAFSA and the CSS Profile. Usually, this will ask similar questions to the other forms, but sometimes it includes unique questions. As stated earlier, your answers must be consistent with other forms submitted.

Even more forms

More forms may be needed, if the following are applicable:

- Divorced/separated parents—the schools may want to know more about your ex-spouse and their financial resources.

- Business forms—the schools may want to learn more about your businesses, especially the financial details. These additional forms are extremely confusing and complex.

Why so many financial aid forms?

Although the FAFSA, CSS Profile, and institutional forms have some unique questions, many of the basic questions are asked three times (cash in bank, investments, etc.). Why? This is either to get you to create a red flag or give up.

"Red flags"

Imagine this scenario: the parent does not get involved with the college process and, in particular, does not complete the financial aid forms. Instead, the student attempts to complete them. The student completes a FAFSA that includes $10K parent cash and $20K parent investments (they just put a number in there to get the task done). Later, the student finds out they have to complete another form and now puts in completely different amounts—let's say, $20K parent cash and $40K parent investments.

The consequence? This creates a "red flag." Now, the financial aid office may ask for six months of bank statements or brokerage account statements to "prove" which numbers are correct. Why? Because they can—they are the gatekeepers.

Give up

Remember, one "myth" you may have heard is: "No matter what, you will never get *free* money." Once you are faced with completing all of these forms, you may remember this and decide to give up and not bother with the headache of completing them. This would be a huge mistake, leading to missed opportunities.

My recommended insights are:

- Always tell the truth.

- Make sure numbers on *all* forms are consistent (to avoid "red flags").

- *Never* give up—get through the process; it will pay off.

I provide more details regarding the forms and the process of getting them done later; however, right now I want to present you with more important information to grasp at this point.

Financial aid form mistakes

What if you make a mistake? It could cost you thousands—even tens of thousands—of dollars.

Because the forms are so complex and confusing, there is a potential to make mistakes, but how would you ever know you made a mistake? All you will get is an SAI number output from the black box. Consider this example:

Remember, the SAI reduction strategy explained in Chapter 10 where $40K in college savings in the student's name has an SAI charge of about $10K; whereas, if in the parents' names (legally), it has an SAI charge of about $2K—an $8K difference? Keep that in mind using the following example.

If you had a $40K 529 plan, is it a student or a parent asset? Because it has a student's name on the account (and to get the tax benefit), it must be used for that student's college costs to optimize the tax benefit. Therefore, many people would consider it a student asset and put the dollar amounts in the student asset box on the forms. The vast majority of 529 plans—wherein the parent is the owner and the student is listed as the beneficiary—would actually be considered a parent asset in the financial aid formulas. If a $40K 529 plan asset was set up this way and mistakenly put as a student asset, the result would be an $8K mistake! Would you even know you made an $8K mistake. Or any other mistakes?

When should you submit forms?

On this topic, there are three common myths about when to complete the forms:

- October of senior year

- After you get accepted by the college

- After your tax returns are done

Why fill in the forms in October?

In a typical year, the FAFSA form is made available to the public on 1 October for new high school seniors and their families; therefore, many people assume that is the due date. As you have learned, there are many other forms besides the FAFSA to be completed. Plus, even if you submitted a FAFSA in early October, the school would not look at it until much later; in most cases, many months later.

New FAFSA (proposed FAFSA "simplification")

To make things worse, as mentioned previously, the Department of Education has now announced that the new FAFSA will be delayed until December 2023. Assuming that this deadline is met, plus there are no major launch issues, that will create even more confusion than in a "normal" year.

Please double-check what the current situation is, get informed, and plan accordingly. Despite all of this, the fundamental idea of finding the most free money from your right schools does *not* change.

Why fill in the forms after you have been accepted?

Many would assume a student would not be considered for financial aid until after the child is accepted at the college. In fact, for most schools, the financial aid forms deadlines are typically soon after their application deadlines—this is especially true for schools with money.

Why fill in the forms after a completed tax return?

Many questions on the financial aid forms explicitly refer to items on an actual federal tax return; but you cannot fill in these forms until the tax return is done. Unfortunately, schools do not care whether you complete your tax return or not. If you have not, they expect you to put in estimates by their deadlines. (An interesting note—this used to be a huge issue. Just a few years ago you needed estimates, but now most people can use actual figures.)

My recommended insights

All of the above answers are wrong. As a result, there could be huge financial consequences if you miss school deadlines.

Every school is unique, therefore for each college applied to, you must:

- Determine the school's financial aid process
- Find out which forms the school requires
- Learn their deadlines and do *not* miss them

To make this even more complicated, schools have different deadlines if you are applying early decision/

action vs. regular decision. You must be aware of these factors too, if applicable.

More details on the financial aid form process

The following checklists contain more detailed steps needed to complete each type of form.

FAFSA checklist

- Apply or obtain FSA ID from the FAFSA website.

- Gather the documents needed.

- Submit your FAFSA (and other forms) on time.

- Retrieve or review your Student Aid Report (SAR).

- Correct any mistakes, if applicable.

- Comply with any additional information requests from the school.

- Be proactive with the financial aid office at the school.

When I say "be proactive," I mean do not assume that you have completed/submitted all the relevant forms. Contact each school to verify that all required forms have been received; if not, correct any deficiencies ASAP.

CSS Profile checklist

- Register for the CSS Profile on the CollegeBoard website.

- Gather the documents needed.

- Submit your CSS Profile (and other forms) on time.

- Don't forget any supplemental questions.

- Comply with any additional information requests from the school.

- Be proactive with the financial aid office at the school.

Additional forms

Be aware of any additional forms, including:

- Business/farm forms

- Separation/divorce (non-custodial) forms

- Federal government verification

You're not done yet

Assuming you have met all the requirements and submitted all the required financial aid forms for each school, you now have to wait to find out if your student has been accepted at each school. If they have—meaning you have received a letter of acceptance from the school's admissions office—you now have to focus your attention on the school's financial aid office.

At this stage, I urge you to be proactive. Do not assume everything is fine and will just happen. Remember, you need to submit financial aid forms to get the financial aid office involved. As a result, you will ultimately get a financial aid award letter from the college. Contact the financial aid office and ask when you can expect to receive this letter, then keep track of the dates and make sure you get it.

Finalize the award

Now that you have received your financial aid award letter, there's even more to do. Here is an overview of additional terms and/or steps you will be exposed to or expected to complete:

- IRS Data Retrieval
- IRS Transcript
- IDOC
- Copies of federal tax returns, W-2s, 1099s, etc.
- Copies of business tax returns, etc., if applicable

Be aware that once you receive your award letter, it will typically say (somewhere in the fine print) that the award letter is an estimate. Although there may be other requests for certain information, the key thing for you to realize is the school will be asking for your income tax filing information to verify that the income information you put on your financial aid forms is reasonably accurate. Your award will not be final until you submit this required information.

Unfortunately, each school will ask for this information in different ways. Some schools will automatically verify your tax information on your FAFSA based on something called an IRS Data Retrieval tool (where the information is directly transmitted by the IRS onto your FAFSA filing).

Unfortunately, private schools are different. They may ask you to sign an IRS Transcript, which is a form that authorizes the school to ask for a copy of your tax return. Others simply ask for you to make copies of tax returns, etc. to send directly to them.

The other major option is something called IDOC, where the school asks you to send the forms to a third-party vendor, who, in turn, scans them and submits them to the school.

In any case, be proactive. Do not assume the school has everything.

Analyze financial aid awards

In a perfect world, you now have all of your kid's acceptances and financial aid award letters. It's time to analyze your awards.

The first thing to be aware of is, unfortunately, not all of the schools will send you award letters at the same time. Further, what if you are waitlisted or deferred? There can be some complex timing situations to navigate through.

To keep it relatively simple, what I generally advise is if you want to get the most free money from schools, you need to be patient and try to get all of the award letters you can so you can analyze all of the awards "apples to apples."

The other complicating factor is that the award letters can be somewhat confusing, what I call "in a foreign language." As I stated earlier, I consider financial aid to be *free* money you do not have to pay back. Unfortunately, colleges generally do not agree with me. Therefore, your financial aid package may include loans (that you or the student will have to pay back) and/or a campus job (where the student has to earn the money). Many prestigious schools do this, which is extremely disappointing as it may mislead you into making a huge mistake. So, be careful to identify which parts of the awards are actually *free* money (typically noted as grants or scholarships) vs. something else.

Assuming you are careful, another important task is to now compare the "true costs" of each school "side by side." In effect, you want to come up with total cost of attendance (or sticker price, including "toothpaste, laundry detergent, and an occasional pizza"), and then subtract the free money to come up with true costs "apples to apples."

One thing I see way too often is a student gets accepted at a private school and receives the XYZ scholarship for $40K. The parent is so proud of this achievement and boasts about it around town. What may not be fully understood is that the scholarship is actually $40K for all four years combined, therefore only $10K per year. Let's say another school awards the ABC scholarship for $120K; you quickly figure out that is $30K/year and still boast about it around town. What if the school's sticker price is $80K, but the family did not realize that? Therefore, the true cost will actually be $50K ($80K minus $30K *free*) and the family budget was only $30–35K. That could be an unpleasant surprise once the bill is due.

College cost comparison sheet

Below is a sample view of a tool to help you analyze the true costs, plus out-of-pocket costs of each school, once you apply the financial aid awards to each school's cost of attendance. The intent is to get a true "apples to apples" comparison of the schools' net prices per year.

College Cost Comparison Worksheet

Student name: _____

The following schedule will help you determine the true cost of each college, and which college award will provide the least out-of-pocket expense to your family. Record the total amount of each category (grants, loans, work study) for every award letter, and compare the results for each college.

COLLEGE	A Total cost of college	B Total grants/ scholarships	C Total work study	D[1] Total loans	E[2] "True" cost	F[3] Family out-of-pocket expense
	$	$	$	$	$	$
	$	$	$	$	$	$
	$	$	$	$	$	$
	$	$	$	$	$	$
	$	$	$	$	$	$
	$	$	$	$	$	$
	$	$	$	$	$	$
	$	$	$	$	$	$

(1) Do not include PLUS loans in this total: only student loans (typically $5,500 Direct/Stafford)
(2) "True cost" (E) = A − B
(3) Family out-of-pocket expenses (F) = A − (B + C + D)

Summary

Free money isn't going to fall into your lap or miraculously appear in your bank account. You must diligently go through the financial aid processes for each school. To apply for aid, you must fill out the FAFSA for all schools; the CSS Profile and school institutional forms for most private schools; plus any additional forms (for example, for separated parents or businesses). You need to be careful to fill in the same financial information across all forms consistently to avoid "red flags," and keep going, even though the forms can be complicated—never give up. It is worth doing your research to work out each individual college's financial aid process, forms required, and deadlines to submit the forms for optimal results.

Once you have been accepted and have your financial aid letter from each college, make sure to finalize your award, following the steps explained above. Next, take the time to analyze all of your awards "apples to apples" to ensure you are getting the most *free* money. Use the cost comparison worksheet given in this chapter to get an overview of each school's net prices per year.

Now that you have all of these options, what do you do next? If you have done everything properly thus far, and have lots of great options, we recommend you negotiate for a better deal. Read on…

12
... Then Negotiate

Did you know colleges would rather make a deal than have empty seats?

Doing a deal

Once you have a good idea of what kinds of schools are right for your student, you need to pick the schools that are acceptable to your student and that you can afford. If you have analyzed all of your financial aid awards using my suggested college cost comparison sheet from the previous chapter, you should have a good idea what each school's true cost is. Now let's explore another huge opportunity—negotiating.

In normal economic times, when buying a car, do you pay sticker price or make a deal with the car dealer? The latter, right? Well, that same analogy is true for colleges.

Imagine I am the CFO at one of the schools you are targeting. Here are my priorities:

- I need to pay the bills: professors, staff, utilities, etc.

- The worst thing for me is an empty seat (lack of students attending the school and paying the fees).

- Therefore, I am willing to give a discount (in the form of financial aid) so your student comes.

- Any revenue vs. $0 is good.

- Plus, I'm willing to make a deal, i.e., negotiate.

Who knew? Therein lies another opportunity that the vast majority of families are missing and one of the reasons why I have written this book—don't be scared off by the initial financial aid offer.

The negotiation process

How would you like to get even more of other people's money? More *free* money from the schools themselves? The answer is to negotiate, for the following reasons:

- Some schools mis-award (make mistakes).

- Some schools under-award (on purpose).

- Some schools are willing to match other schools' awards.

- You should know whether or not to accept the first award letter.

- You should learn how to talk to the people in the financial aid office.

The negotiation process is an often overlooked and underappreciated part of the college process. Schools are available and willing to discuss their offers with you. There are, at times, mistakes made, things over-looked, or circumstances that need to be explained. This is your opportunity to have a voice. The relatively small investment of time on your part could reap large rewards—even *more* free money.

Schools make mistakes. One situation I had with a client was a child had been accepted at a 100% need-based school with (at the time) a sticker price of $65K, and a need of $30K and the school did not offer them anything. If they did not know any better, they may have assumed, "Oh well, we did not get any help and therefore we cannot afford the school," and, as a result, gone somewhere else that appeared to cost far less. In this case, with my guidance my client went through a negotiation process focusing on their confusion regarding their need-based aid policy. As a result, the school recognized their mistake and awarded them the $30K+! Do not let this happen to you.

Some schools will give you a low offer and hope you simply take it. Most people never bother to ask for more. Do not let that be you.

If you followed my earlier advice on picking schools that will give you a great deal, you can use that offer to get *more* free money from your schools of choice. Why? Remember my common sense example in Chapter 4? If I am a CFO of a school, I do not want an empty seat; therefore, I am willing to make a deal.

Ultimately, the key is to learn how to talk to those people. Let me give you some ideas.

Talking points template

Presented below is what I call a "talking points" negotiation template. As discussed later, this can be ultimately put in the form of a letter.

SAMPLE NEGOTIATION LETTER

Introduction

Thank you for your recent financial aid award letter and generous award. [College name] is [student's name's] #1 choice—their dream school! [Add personal reasons why this school in particular is #1] However, we are confused and concerned about the amount of aid provided and how we can afford to have [student's name] attend your great school.

If our calculations are correct, we would have to pay and/ or borrow about [$XXX] per year [the true cost from the college cost comparison sheet], or about [$XXX] [the true cost for one year multiplied by four] over four years—a lot of money, and we frankly do not know how we can afford it. Could you please help us?

Optional points:

- **If need-based aid**

As per the U.S. Department of Education, "financial need" = "cost of attendance" – "student aid index" (SAI). Therefore, our assumption was that if we have need, we would get help equal to that. Per our calculations, [student's name's] financial need is [$XXX] (based on cost at [college name] [$XXX] [total "sticker price" from college cost comparison sheet] – our SAI of [$XXX]). However, as per your award letter, we received only [$XXX] [the amount of free money awarded by the school from the college cost comparison sheet]—a difference of [$XXX]!

- **"Average" award**

Further, per CollegeData.com, the "average freshman award" at [college name] is [$XXX] [get that amount from website]. We only received [$XXX]—a difference of [$XXX]. We may be biased, but we feel our son/daughter is at least average—therefore, we expected more.

- **Other schools**

Also, we can go to other schools for less. For example, [student's name] can go to [School Y] for [$XXX], [School Z]... [true costs from other schools on college cost *comparison sheet]. As parents that must pay the bills, these differences add up to a lots of money—especially over four years!*

- **Special circumstances (sob story) examples**
  - ○ Financial (lost job, catastrophe, etc.)
  - ○ Other children in college/grad school
  - ○ Other children going to college in future
  - ○ Multiple residences due to work

Summary

Thank you for your consideration. Anything you can do to help us make this financial decision easier, plus allow us to let [student's name] attend their #1 choice would be greatly appreciated.

Please feel to contact me directly if I can answer any questions or be of any assistance.

Sincerely,

[Signed parent's name]

Key points about the template

This template should cover most situations. Simply use the points that are applicable to you:

- The introduction is focusing on "I need your help as I am confused by the amount of award," avoiding using the words "negotiate" or "appeal."

- *If* you are eligible for need-based aid, use that section; if not, simply skip that point.

- The "sob story" section is where you get to add your personalized situation. I have provided a couple of typical scenarios as examples.

- The summary is once again focused on "I need your help"—just like the introduction.

Negotiation strategies

Here is an overview of our recommended negotiation process:

- When all acceptance letters and financial aid packages are received, complete a college cost comparison worksheet (see Chapter 11) to give an indication of the "true cost" to attend each college.

- Be proactive.

- Personalize and customize the "talking points" template to your own unique situation.

Ideally, approach the financial aid office directly and request a face-to-face meeting ASAP:

- Memorize your "talking points"—be prepared.

- Insist on speaking with someone in authority. Don't be satisfied until you have spoken to the

head of department. If you are not satisfied,
be persistent.

- Be respectful and courteous—you are seeking
  help, not fighting a battle.

- Avoid words like "negotiate," "appeal," etc. You
  are confused by their offer and seeking help.

The alternative is to convert your "talking points"
into a letter requesting help:

- The "talking points" are organized as paragraphs
  of a letter—just follow the order presented.

- Address the letter to:
  - The person's name on the financial aid
    award letter from the college's financial
    aid department.
  - If no name is given, look up the head of the
    financial aid department in that college and
    address the letter to that person.
  - In the reference line, put the student's name
    and either the college ID number (if supplied)
    or the social security number.

- Fax the letter directly and call the financial aid
  office to request a telephone meeting ASAP to
  discuss the contents.

- Less desirable is to proactively fax the letter
  (with an email and/or snail mail backup) and
  request feedback.

If you are not happy or satisfied with the initial response, I recommend escalating it to "a supervisor" or ultimately to the head of the financial aid department, if necessary. You want to get a definitive final answer so you can make the "right" school decision.

Summary

You may not be comfortable with negotiating or feel it's an area in which you have little experience. Don't let that deter you. By negotiating, you are expanding the opportunities to send your kid to the right school for them and for a better price.

There are many reasons why you should negotiate with your chosen schools: mistakes are made, things can be overlooked, or circumstances may need to be explained. Use this opportunity to have a voice, adapting the "talking points" letter template to your own circumstances, and following our recommended negotiation strategy steps to speak to the right person in the financial aid department. If you are respectful, courteous, and persistent, colleges (especially those with money) will respond.

PART FIVE
WHAT NEXT?

13
Your Options

Did you know there is an overwhelming amount of information out there regarding the college selection process?

The next steps

Now that you have been educated and informed about how to *Pay for College Without Going Broke*, what are your next steps?

In this chapter, I am going to provide you with various options and resources (besides this book) that you may be exposed to or learn about from friends, family, and neighbors. I will also candidly assess their potential value and relative usefulness to you. Then, in the next chapter, I will provide you with my recommendations of what you need to do besides utilizing the guidance provided—an action plan.

School data options

At this stage, the questions I am typically asked are:

- Where can I find a list of the right schools for my pocketbook?

- Which schools have more money than others?

- Which schools are 100% need-based?

- Which schools give tuition discounts?

What you need are resources that give you specific school data for every school as follows:

- The average free financial aid award

- The percentage of students that receive *free* money

Even better, you need data that breaks down awards into need-based vs. non-need-based (merit) and data that is sorted as lists of schools by aid type. For example, if you are looking for 100% need-based schools, you would want to find a list of those, with:

- Percentage of need met

- Percentage of need met with *free* money

- Average need-based aid *free* money award

If you are never going to get need-based aid, you would want to avoid 100% need-based schools. Instead, you would want a list of tuition discount schools. Those would be schools that give a high percentage of students' merit aid and provide a large average amount of merit aid. In particular:

- Percentage of students receiving non-need-based aid

- Average non-need-based aid *free* money award

The bad news is that in my more than twenty years' experience (and going back to my high school days), I have never seen these types of lists publicly available. In fact, even finding the data on a school-by-school basis is difficult. There are numerous books and websites with information on college planning—even how to complete financial aid forms line by line—but not this type of school data needed in a useful format.

Yet what is interesting is that this data *does* exist; in fact, both the Federal Department of Education and other third parties collect the data every year from colleges. Organizations such as Barron's, CollegeBoard/ BigFuture, The Princeton Review, and other websites publish various pieces of this data; but not in a format I believe is useful.

What I ultimately recommend for readers is to find a college planning specialist that focuses on knowing which schools provide more *free* money than others for a family's unique situation. Those folks have accumulated the right data, created their own databases, and can sort the data in a variety of ways.

I'll come back to college planning specialists shortly. Meanwhile, let me provide various school data options that you will learn about or discover on your own.

College books and websites

As mentioned earlier, there are many books and websites by major publishers regarding colleges (Barron's, Princeton Review, etc.) These are the giant books you would see in the college section of major bookstores and online booksellers (in recent years, publishers are no longer printing these books like they used to). These same publishers also have websites that provide data.

The positives: On the plus side, there is lots of data about each school, typically including a section on financial aid.

The negatives: The financial aid data, however, is typically generic; for example, it may say "X% of all freshmen receive some form of financial aid," and "the average award is $Y." Assuming this is statistically correct, how does it apply to your unique situation? If you have need, you may prefer schools that provide 100% need met with *free* money. This generic information is not specific enough to tell you which school is which.

(However, I do recommend one particular book that all of you should get right away. It is called the *Fiske Guide to Colleges*;[38] more about it in the next chapter.)

CollegeBoard/BigFuture

A special comment on what was CollegeBoard but is currently called BigFuture.[39] This used to be a great resource for online school data. For every school, it had a section called "Paying for College." Within the tabs, you could get detailed information about need-based aid and merit aid, which provided a pretty good indication of what kind of aid package you were likely to get at the school. Further, the data was updated every year (it would disclose which year the data was sourced) and was reasonably current.

For some reason, a couple of years ago, they revamped their website and all the data in that format is no longer provided. Instead, they provide something called

---

38   EB Fiske, *Fiske Guide to Colleges 2023* (Sourcebooks, 2022)
39   BigFuture, https://bigfuture.collegeboard.org, accessed 18 September 2023

average net price, plus some other statistical data. To me, an average net price is meaningless as it is far too general. Further, it is not clear how current the data is. I do not find this website as useful as it used to be.

CollegeData.com

As an alternative to BigFuture, CollegeData.com[40] is a good resource.

The positives: There is a lot of data about each school, including a detailed "financials" section. This contains useful statistics on financial aid, which will give you a pretty good idea of what types of aid they provide and how much. Also, the information is presented in a relatively summarized way, which is fairly easy to understand.

The negatives: The data is not kept as current as the data CollegeBoard used to provide, but they do disclose which year it comes from.

College Navigator

A great new resource I recently discovered that literally has all kinds of college data in *lots* of detail is College Navigator, which can be found on the

---

40 CollegeData.com, http://collegedata.com, accessed 18 September 2023

National Center for Education Statistics (NCES) website.[41] For those that are looking for lots of detailed information, school by school, including financial aid data and admission statistics, NCES is a more detailed version of what CollegeBoard used to be, with more details than you can find on CollegeData.com.

The positives: This would be the best resource to use if you are going to do detailed research. It is a free resource with an amazing amount of detailed information, school by school, plus the ability to do all kinds of customized "searches" using their search engine.

The negatives: It does not appear to break down financial aid into need-based vs. merit, which to me is a critical data point, but I would still recommend this as a great starting point for your research. The other negative is that as it is *so* detailed, it may be too overwhelming to navigate through.

Net price calculators

Some years ago, the Federal Department of Education required all colleges and universities to put what is called a net price calculator (NPC) on their college websites. The idea was to provide some transparency of what the net cost may be for a given student that gets accepted at that school. This is something to explore as an option.

---

41 National Center for Education Statistics, www.nces.ed.gov, accessed 18 September 2023

The positives: The NPC calculation is based on your unique inputs—for example, a student's grades and test scores, parents' and student's financial information (income, assets, etc.). In theory, it should give you a good idea of how much free money you will receive from that school to get to the net cost.

The negatives: Unfortunately, theory is different to reality. Be wary of the results from an NPC.

First, the Department of Education regulated that the NPCs must be on each school's website, but did not provide a meaningful oversight on whether the net prices shown are realistic. Sad to say, many schools will provide an optimistic, even misleading, net price vs. the actual final net cost after getting accepted and receiving any financial aid.

Second, have you heard the phrase "garbage in, garbage out" in the IT world? This means if the data input into the calculation is incorrect, the output will be wrong. The most difficult portion of the inputs on the NPC is the financial inputs. Most people are not familiar with the terms and simply make mistakes. The problem is, you may never know you have made a mistake, which may dramatically affect the output.

Common Data Set

For many years, the Federal Department of Education has collected information annually from colleges themselves in the form of what is called a common data set (CDS). The overall CDS is an overwhelming amount of data; however, the financial aid data portion captures this data in a format needed to determine which schools provide which types of financial aid (need-based vs. merit) and how much. This includes breakdowns of free money vs. loans, etc. Finding this data would be the best resource for what you need on a school-by-school basis, if readily available.

The positives: Many schools put their detailed CDS on their website. If you can find it, you will have access to the data you need to get a great idea of what type of financial aid school it is, and how much free aid is provided per typical student.

The negatives: Unfortunately, not all schools provide links to their detailed CDS, or if they do it is not readily clear where the data is. Further, even if provided, the data can be in a format that is extremely confusing to decipher.

College Aid Pro

A nice resource I recently discovered is College Aid Pro.[42] This is the best resource available to the public I have found to date.

---

42 College Aid Pro, https://collegeaidpro.com, accessed 18 September 2023

The positives: The primary focus of their website is to pay less for college, with an emphasis on learning about free money from colleges rather than loans. It has a lot of good educational materials and access to college financial data at a useful, detailed level. It also includes access to a college search (of their database), based on an affordability profile that is unique to your situation. Even though you are still "doing it yourself," this option provides you access to school data in a more comprehensive, user-friendly way.

The negatives: To get access to the most useful, robust features of their online tool, you will have to upgrade for a modest monthly and/or annual fee. However, you can try it out for free.

Other resources

As you can see, there are lots of options to find school data out there, although the data needed is generally not easy to find or is in a format that is not useful. Further, all the above options will require you to research the data for each school one by one. That is quite a tedious process, even if you can find the data in a useful format. As of the writing of this book, I would recommend College Aid Pro as the best public resource for this data I have discovered to date.

Ideally, you want to find someone (or a group) that can help you with all of items outlined in my ideal approach, and the areas focused on in this book. For example:

- How can I find a college that I can afford?

- Which are the right schools for me?

- Which schools will solve my matrix for my unique college planning situation?

- How can I get more *free* money?

High school guidance departments

I am a big fan of high school guidance departments and counselors. Sadly, however, over the last twenty to thirty years, budgets and resources for guidance departments— in particular, guidance counselors— have been severely cut, meaning this service is stretched way too thin. In fact, they will readily admit they do not have resources to help on the financial side (versus admissions/academic), and typically there are thousands of kids assigned to each counselor. If you are not sure, ask your child's counselor how much personal one-on-one time they can provide to your student (or yourself).

At the same time, don't overlook this resource. Find out what your high school guidance department is going to do for your child. How much "one-on-one" time is each of your students getting to navigate through the college planning maze? If you do not know, ask.

Unfortunately, for most of you, resources will be extremely limited and restricted to the academic/admissions side. Will they help with essay critiques? Interview prep? How about standardized tests? For example, did you know that popular SAT test prep group classes range from $1–3K? That is just one small part of where help may be needed in addition to the guidance counselors, and it can add up quickly.

However, if we focus on the free money part, as I outlined in my scattergram example in Chapter 8, the vast majority of high school guidance departments (and their counselors)—even though well-intentioned—are not experts in how to pay for college or how to make college more affordable. Once again, take advantage of any help they could provide, but who else can help?

Tax preparers, accountants, or financial advisors

Remember, I am a CPA. I am not here to pick on accountants; however, in my experience, few accountants are experts in college planning. Consider the following points:

- Typically, accountants that do tax returns are scorekeepers looking at the past; they are generally not forward-looking planners.

- Tax formulas are different than SAI calculations.

- Completing tax returns is different to filling out financial aid forms.

If your accountant, tax preparer, or CPA can help you, take advantage of that expertise. Similarly, in my experience, financial advisors are not experts in college planning. If your financial advisor can help you, you should also use their expertise.

College financial aid counselors

Will financial aid counselors at colleges help you? They may be a potential resource, but consider this: colleges are a big business and, as a result, common sense should suggest they would prefer to give you *less* free money, not more. Further, as described earlier, most parents assume they are not going to get any free money and so never ask for it. Therefore, the colleges probably would not be a good option.

In case you are considering guidance counselors, tax accountants, financial advisors, or the colleges themselves to help you, consider asking them the following questions:

- Can you help me pick schools that will give me the best aid package—meet most need, more free money, less loans, etc.?

- Can you show me how to lower my SAI and maximize my eligibility for aid?

- Can you help me fill out the FAFSA and CSS Profile forms line by line?

- Will you help me negotiate with each school if I get a bad financial aid package or less than I expected?

- Can you show me the best way to pay for college using "my money"?

College planning specialists

What I ultimately recommend you consider as an option is finding a college planning specialist—a professional in a little known but important niche.

There are lots of "college planners" out there. At a minimum, what you want to find is someone who can actually solve your matrix and find the right school for your unique situation. Further, wouldn't it be great if you can find someone that can help you with everything outlined in my ideal approach?

For now, please realize that outside professional help can become costly. Be aware that on the academic/applications side alone, prices range from a few hundred dollars for essay help to $10–30K+ per student. SAT test prep classes and tutors are potential additional costs of thousands of dollars. Relatively few college admissions counselors focus on the financial side—they assume you are going to pay the college bill, whatever the cost.

Imagine then adding costs for financial help too. At this point, realize there are lots of options and resources to consider. If not convinced yet, you can see why the college planning process here in the US is such a confusing, complicated maze—especially for the ill-informed.

Summary

It's easy to get overwhelmed by the amount of information out there, from college books and websites, net price calculators, and the CDS, to trying to find assistance—be it high school guidance departments, tax preparers, accountants, or financial advisors. Each resource has their positives and negatives, but you will need to focus on which can actually solve your matrix and find the right school for your unique situation, using the advice given in this chapter.

Let's now move on to my recommended action plan. In the next chapter, I will discuss college planning specialists in more detail, including a list of questions to ask a potential college planning specialist.

14
Your Action Plan

Did you know most people do not even
know college planning specialists and other
resources exist?

Now that you are armed with information, I am
going to provide you with my recommendations
of what you need to do from here to maximize your
college success—an action plan.

Get the *Fiske Guide to Colleges*

The first thing I recommend is to make sure you get the
most recent *Fiske Guide to Colleges*. I provide this book
to all my client families and tell them to keep it in their
kitchen as a ready reference, as it is a great starting

point to learn about differences among schools—a critical first step in finding the right schools.

Information is provided for about 300 of the "top" schools in the USA (along with some foreign schools), in a format that I find extremely useful and insightful. It provides information in a written essay form, highlighting each school's unique qualities, plus lots of other useful information. (This is an improvement on most other publishers' books and websites, which provide a bunch of "data" and statistics presented in a non-user-friendly way.) This is the best resource to start thinking about the "right" schools and to learn the differences among them.

Why keep it in the kitchen? I typically cite two reasons:

1. If you give it to your college-bound student, it will end up in their room under a pile of clothes, never to be seen again.

2. If you have it in the kitchen, each of you may look at it occasionally with a cup of tea or coffee, based on schools you hear about on your own or schools you learn about from others.

Find a college planning specialist

My second but most important recommendation is to find a college planning specialist who is right for you. Let me repeat what I said in the previous chapter: college planning specialists are professionals in a little known but important niche. Now that you have learned what's possible, why miss out? Wouldn't it be great if you could find someone that could help you with everything outlined in my ideal approach—in effect, "outsource" this to the right person or team? After all, do you solve your own legal or medical problems? Why not seek a "guru" who can save you lots of time and effort, plus ultimately give you "peace of mind," so you don't mess this up for your child?

If finding a school for your student you never thought you could afford or simply saving lots of money is a goal, finding the right specialist may well be worth the upfront investment. Imagine saving thousands, even tens of thousands, per year compared to the cost of the specialist's services—now that's a real "return on investment." And that's in the first year alone; how about over four years?

Now that you are aware of them, do your research and discover specialists that you can consider for your unique situation. As a person who has been doing this for more than twenty years, I urge you to carry out your due diligence. There are lots of "college planners" out there—what you need to do is find the *right* one.

Questions to ask a potential college planning specialist

Using my ideal approach as a guide, will the specialist help to:

1. Pick the right school for your student?

   - Self-discovery / assessments

   - Career research

   - College searches

   - College visits

   - Best fit

   - Provide options

2. Properly prepare / position the student to get accepted at colleges?

   - Specialize in college admissions

   - Provide a proactive roadmap / checklist of tasks

   - Build the Resume of Achievement

   - Provide standardized test strategy / prep

   - Help with essay strategy, critiques, and prep

   - Provide guidance on interview strategies, mock interviews, and prep

3. Provide guidance on getting through the admissions/application process in time?

   - Provide an overall roadmap/checklist of tasks

   - Give advice on deadlines/procedures for each school

   - Track applications/supplements

   - Monitor progress

4. Find the right school for your pocketbook?

   - Calculate SAI

   - Find schools with free money (solve the matrix)

   - Identify need-based vs. non-need-based schools, as appropriate

   - Provide options

5. Provide guidance on getting through the financial aid process in time?

   - Provide an overall roadmap/checklist of tasks

   - Review and/or complete all financial aid forms—FAFSA/CSS Profile, etc.

   - Give advice on deadlines/procedures for each school

   - Track applications/supplements

   - Monitor progress

- Analyze financial aid awards

- Help negotiate with schools

- Give advice on college loan options

6. Develop a comprehensive college funding plan?

- Look at other people's money vs. your money

- Develop a college budget

- Provide options

- Research SAI reduction strategies, if appropriate

- Advise on how to best pay the college bill

- Navigate financial chessboard options

Ask for references and vet them thoroughly. You want to make sure that there is a track record of real success, not just a bunch of empty promises. Be wary of any resource that is unwilling to provide you with references that you can actually speak to.

If you find the right college planning specialist, you should be in great hands. There should be a unique game plan customized to you and your situation—including "getting to know you" (your student, yourself, and your financial situation and goals), lots of information and guidance provided, plus open communication throughout the process.

What if you can't find one?

What if you can't find a college planning specialist in your area? When I started more than twenty years ago, having someone local was extremely important; in fact, my college practice was limited locally to NJ clients. Over time, due to technology (like Zoom), clients were willing to work with me and my team "virtually." As a result, we have helped families nationwide; and yes, even from overseas! Now, due to COVID19, more and more people are used to virtual meetings, so I recommend you consider "expanding your horizons," if needed. Whatever you do, take the time to find a specialist that will save you lots of money.

A "team" of resources

What if you can only find resources that do some of the services that you require? In this case, you may need to create a "team" of resources, rather than a "one-stop shop." Just make sure you have resources for everything you need. Remember what I stated earlier: "You must do all of the steps in my ideal approach in a comprehensive way—if you mess up one it may jeopardize your overall college plan success rate."

How can you build this "team"?

As a preferred second option, your "team" could be a college planning specialist that does the college financial steps only (the parents' journey), not any academic/admissions counseling services. In that case, if you could find a "college admission counselor" who does all the academic/admissions services needed (the student's journey), that would be great!

What if you must build your team with more pieces? Outlined below are my recommendations (once again, using the ideal approach, but broken up into some logical major pieces). I will start with the financial side first (parents) and then the academic/admissions side (the student).

Financial (parents)

Let me start with the most important one: solving your matrix.

Solving your matrix

No matter what you do, you *must* find the right information and/or resources to "solve your matrix"—meaning finding the "right schools for your pocketbook." Figuring out which schools have money, and which match your unique financial situation, is the least understood part of the whole ideal approach. This surprising lack of information is what drove me to start my college planning practice, and what ultimately prompted me to write this book. Based on my experience, these specialists are the hardest to find, plus most families do not even realize they exist.

First and foremost, find a professional specialist that truly knows which schools have money and which don't. Remember, these are the questions to ask for this resource—can you help find the right school for my pocketbook, to:

- Calculate SAI

- Find schools with free money (solve the matrix)

- Identify need-based vs. non-need-based schools, as appropriate

- Provide options

In a similar way to finding an overall college planning specialist, ask for references and vet them thoroughly.

If you find this resource, you then must build the rest of your team based on additional services needed (completing financial aid forms, negotiation, academic counseling, and so on).

College Aid Pro

If for some reason you cannot find this professional resource, I recommend you check out College Aid Pro, who provide a great online tool to help you find schools based on your unique financial situation and the type of schools your child is interested in. Here is an overview of how it works.

It asks for the following inputs:

- Basic information about all family members (such as dates of birth), including the student, parents, siblings, etc.

- The student's achievements: HS GPA, SAT / ACT test scores

- The desired college major

- A current college list (if any)

- Parents' and student's basic financial data: income from last tax returns, assets, debts, etc.

As a result of inputs, College Aid Pro provides:

- A calculated SAI, for both Federal and Institutional Methodology.

- A calculated projected "net cost" per school (if schools were inputted). Its algorithm considers your child's grades and scores, your SAIs, and school scholarships (need-based and non-need-based, as appropriate).

Although it is not perfect, it is the best current online tool I have found to give you a pretty good approximation of how much free money you are going to get (or not), based on the schools you provided.

What's even better, there all kinds of searches, sorts, and other queries you can do of its "database" to find other schools of interest. For example, finding schools that have the lowest net cost for your student in a certain region of the country, a particular college major, or ranked in the top 100 academically. Pretty robust! Further, you can drill down school by school and see detailed information about each one, including whether they give lots of need-based or non-need-based aid.

Financial aid process

Another important member of your "team" would be finding those that get you through the financial aid process. Ideally, this would include assisting you with completing *all* of the financial aid forms required, plus assisting with negotiations and college loan options.

Remember, these are the questions to ask for this resource—can you help:

- Provide guidance on getting through the financial aid process in time?
    - Overall roadmap/checklist of tasks
    - Review and/or complete all financial aid forms—FAFSA/CSS Profile, etc.

- Give advice on deadlines/procedures for each school

- Track applications/supplements

- Monitor progress

- Analyze financial aid awards

- Help negotiate with schools

- Give advice on college loan options

The first group I would seek are professional "college financial aid specialists" that ideally focus on all of these tasks. Let me distinguish this group from another group called "college funding specialists," which I will describe later. In many cases, you may find aid specialists that help with the forms only, but do not help you with the rest of the steps. If that is the case, I recommend you find at least a "financial aid form" specialist and a "negotiation" specialist. If you able to find those two resources, the rest of the work you need to do largely involves checking out each school's website to determine which forms are required and the deadlines for each one. Simply organizing those tasks yourself can work in a pinch.

There are many "college financial aid specialists" out there. As always, be wary. Similar to finding an overall college planning specialist, ask for references and vet them thoroughly. Try not to limit yourself to local only, as many reputable professionals can perform tasks virtually or online.

Don't overlook tax professionals or CPAs. Many of them offer financial aid form assistance as well. Why? Because lots of the information needed comes right off your tax returns.

Comprehensive college planning

The next area of expertise you need on your team is help with developing a comprehensive college funding plan. This is another component of the parents' journey in the ideal approach—what I call "the college financial chessboard."

Remember, these are the questions to ask for this resource—can you help:

- Develop a comprehensive college funding plan?
    - Look at other people's money vs. your money
    - Develop a college budget
    - Provide options
    - Research SAI reduction strategies, if appropriate
    - Advise on how to best pay the college bill
    - Navigate financial chessboard options

The first group I would look for are what I call "professional college funding specialists" that ideally focus on all of these tasks. Let me distinguish this group from the "college financial aid specialists" described above. If you could find resources that do both financial aid and what I call "college funding," that would be preferred; however, in my experience, that combination is rare.

One thing to note is there are many organizations that "certify" college funding specialists. One such group is the National Institute of Certified College Planners (NICCP), which oversees the Certified College Planning Specialist (CCPS) designation— something I obtained some fifteen years ago. That group is worth checking out.

Similar to my other recommendations, there are many "college funding specialists" out there. As always, be wary. Similar to finding an overall college planning specialist, ask for references and vet them thoroughly. Try not to limit yourself to local only, as many reputable professionals can perform tasks virtually or online.

Don't overlook other financial advisors, such as Certified Financial Planners (CFP). Many of them offer college financial planning assistance as well.

Academic (student)

The other important part of your "team" of resources would be those who can help you with finding the "right" school for your student, plus how to get them accepted at their schools of choice. This is essentially the upper left-hand side of the ideal approach document presented earlier—the student's journey.

Remember the questions to ask for this resource—can you help:

- Pick the right school for the student?
    - Self-discovery / assessments
    - Career research
    - College searches
    - College visits
    - Best fit
    - Provide options
- Properly prepare / position the student to get accepted at colleges?
    - Specialize in college admissions
    - Provide a proactive roadmap / checklist of tasks
    - Build the Resume of Achievement
    - Standardized test strategy / prep
    - Help with essay strategy, critiques, and prep
    - Provide guidance on interview strategies, mock interviews, and prep

- Provide guidance on getting through the admissions/application process in time?
    - Provide an overall roadmap/checklist of tasks
    - Give advice on deadlines/procedures for each school
    - Track applications/supplements
    - Monitor progress

High school guidance department

The first thing to do is check out your student's high school guidance department. I provide some overall general information about these folks in the previous chapter; however, every high school is different and has a variety of capabilities and resources available. You need to find out what they are. Are they simply online resources (like a popular tool used by many called "Naviance" with little personal guidance, or lots of one-on-one help)?

You also need to find out what your high school guidance department is going to do specifically for your child. If unsure, ask your child's counselor how much personal one-on-one time they can provide to your child (or yourself). Some schools provide resources to handle all the "questions to ask" out-lined above—including test prep classes and essay writing workshops; others do not. Once again, now that you are informed about what you need to do, assess whether the school provides enough help and whether you need other supplemental pieces of your "team" from somewhere else.

Another important consideration is to truly determine whether your child will need professional guidance (please do not get offended when I say they may "need a babysitter") or can work independently with minimal supervision to guide them step-by-step through all of these processes.

Trust me, I know this is a lot of work to check out, but it is critically important. In my experience, many parents simply "assume" that all of these things are taken care of by the school. Please do not assume so—it will cost you.

What if the high school can only help you with some things and not all? Once again, you may need to find other resources to complement the high school capabilities.

Professional admissions counselors

Besides the high school guidance department counselors and resources, the other major area to consider is professional college admissions counselors. There are lots of folks out there that offer "college admission" services, but what are their credentials? If you quickly search the internet for your area or state, you will probably see lots of them. Be wary.

PAY FOR COLLEGE WITHOUT GOING BROKE

I recommend you find professional counselors. There are two predominant professional academic counselor associations I suggest you check out: the National Association of College Admissions Counseling (NACAC)[43] and the Independent Educational Consultants Association (IECA).[44] Most admissions counselors on college campuses, and many high school guidance counselors, are members of one of these two associations.

Look for those that offer their services to individual families. If you simply go to each association's website, you can check out the association, but more importantly you can seek a list of counselors in your area to consider which are of interest to you—each will list their services, areas of expertise, and costs. Whatever you do, check out their references to make sure they will provide the services they say they will, but unique to your needs.

College essays and interviews

Please be aware that most high school guidance departments and even many professional college admissions counselors do not provide help or guidance with college essays or college interviews. Therefore, you may need to seek professional help

---

43 National Association of College Admissions Counseling, https://www.nacacnet.org, accessed 18 September 2023

44 Independent Educational Consultants Association, www.iecaonline.com, accessed 18 September 2023

there as well and add this to your "team." Once again, there are lots of resources and services to research; you must do your due diligence.

A couple of "insights" on essays and interviews. As I mentioned earlier, private colleges typically have a much more robust college admissions process than public schools—including potential requirements for essays and interviews. Why? Because they can.

For every school your student is applying to, you must find out what each school's application requirements are and their deadlines. Each school is different. You may hear about the "common application" and the "common app essay." Many schools require the common app essay; others require even more essays. Therefore, the potential need for help is beyond the high school or other admissions counselors and essay assistance services may range from a blank piece of paper with an essay strategy needed to start, all the way through to a final draft "essay critique." If not clear, they may have to do many essays. Again, find the right help.

College interviews are often misunderstood and/or overlooked. Why? Because, for many schools, they are "optional." In my opinion (and for my clients), they are "required," not optional. To me, it is another opportunity to stand out from the other applicants in the college pool. Preparing for interviews—including doing "mock interviews" (just like preparing for a job interview)—is another college success factor for which other professional resources may be needed.

Test prep

I also want to alert you to another specialized area in the college admissions side: test prep. Most high schools, and most college admissions counselors, do not provide test prep. Therefore, another member of your "team" may be needed.

Currently, the "hot" trend in college admissions is the idea of "SAT optional." What this means is that the trend in recent years is to allow students the option of whether or not to submit standardized test scores. This most recently was driven by COVID19 because test sites were shut down. As a result, colleges were forced to go optional. Post-COVID19, most have not changed their policy and as a result, many students simply skip the tests altogether (an "easy way out"). Now more and more students are applying to many schools they previously would not have applied to because they do not have to worry about inferior scores. This has led to an explosion in college applications, especially at top schools, and the biggest driver of lower acceptance rates (statistics I outlined earlier) in the last couple of years.

Do not fall into this trap. Think about it. If your child does the right test prep and can attain top scores, wouldn't it be beneficial to submit those scores as part of their college applications? Common sense dictates that, once again, that student would stand out against those that did not "optionally" submit test scores—make sense? Therefore, I recommend you prepare for these tests as part of your college admission strategy and plans.

What are my test prep options?

I recommend that your student tries an online test prep option—my favorite being ePrep[45]—before you spend potentially thousands of dollars for test prep classes and/or tutors. If this works, great; you can save lots of money. If it doesn't, you still have other options before it's too late.

Let me quickly outline four different test prep approaches and my condensed analysis (pros/cons) of each.

1. Self-study books

- Pros: Inexpensive.

- Cons: Generic; not customized; student must be disciplined/responsible.

---

45 ePrep, www.eprep.com, accessed 18 September 2023

2. Scheduled classes/courses

- Pros: Provide structure/discipline, if needed.

- Cons: Expensive; typically not customized (like an HS class, may be boring/easy or difficult/ hard); cannot miss classes.

3. Private tutor

- Pros: May be customized; provides schedule/ discipline.

- Cons: May NOT be customized; expensive.

4. Online test prep (ePrep as an example)

- Pros: Relatively inexpensive; flexible schedule (for busy kids); customized based on interaction.

- Cons: Need responsible/disciplined student.

Overall, my recommendation is for your student to set a goal of getting the best test scores possible and submitting them as part of the application process. If so, finding the right test prep is critical.

Lastly, can your student get accepted without submitting test scores? Yes, of course, like many others, but why take that risk? Instead, let's open up the doors to the most "right" schools possible.

Don't forget the internet

Do not overlook the internet for help. There are "experts" on almost any subject available if you look for them. If you're not sure, try a web search like: "How to complete the FAFSA form YouTube" and see what comes up. You will be amazed what's out there. Obviously, now the challenge will be to figure out which expert knows what they are talking about. Clearly, that type of approach would be extremely tedious, but it is doable and it is free.

Remember my personal college journey story? The internet did not even exist but somehow I found enough information to start ("the hard way"). Through persistence and learning along the way, I ultimately made it. Looking back, did I make lots of mistakes? Definitely. I wish I'd had the information I know now, but it did not exist back then, plus I was essentially on my own.

Summary

Doing nothing is not an option. To maximize your college success, follow the action plan above—getting the *Fiske Guide to Colleges*, finding a college planning specialist, and utilizing a team of resources, such as College Aid Pro, the high school guidance department, and professional college admissions counselors—to solve your matrix. You will need help to prepare your student for college essays and interviews as well as test prep, and it pays to know all your options.

You can do it, and this book should provide you with most, if not all, of the information you need to find college success. I wish you the best.

15
What Have We Learned?

Did you know that knowing more gets
you more?

You don't have to settle

In this journey together, we have discovered that a college education and financial security are not mutually
exclusive. You don't have to settle for one or the other;
you can have both. Let's revisit what we have covered
that will enable you to fund college while remaining
within your financial means.

To begin with, there are lots of myths versus realities. I urge you not to rely on friends, family,
and neighbors—however well-intentioned their

advice—for accurate information. Some schools provide more free money than others, and understanding each school's financial policy is critical.

Just like buying a car, a college sticker price means nothing. Most free money comes from the colleges themselves, not from the government or private scholarships. In fact, as we now know, there are billions of financial aid dollars available per year—the key is learning where and how to get it. Colleges are the gatekeepers of over 90% of all financial aid; therefore, you must ask for it by going through the financial aid process.

At the same time, finding your student's best fit (big, small, country, city)—the right school for them—is critical; otherwise, it may cost you. You do not want to have your student go six or seven years to get a four-year degree. Make sure you find the right schools for your pocketbook—schools that you never thought you could afford—by learning how to solve your matrix for your unique college situation.

Finally, the best college financial planning strategy is to get as much other people's (free) money vs. your money as possible. Navigating the financial aid process is not easy, but if you get through it you will be rewarded. There are many financial strategies available to better use your money by playing your financial chessboard.

WHAT HAVE WE LEARNED?

In essence, get educated and informed—knowing more gets you more.

Summary

We now know that the following are all possible. You can:

- Go to schools you never thought you could afford

- Use other people's money vs. your money to help pay for college

- Get tens of thousands of dollars per year from the colleges themselves

- Get *free* money, not loans

- Increase your odds of college success by finding the right school for your student

- Live on campus at a four-year college rather than "going the hard way"

There is plenty of choice out there; you just need to research your options and find the right help for you.

Much of the information covered in this book may have been new, if not surprising, to you. Either way, I hope it has opened up the possibility of a bright future for you and your kids.

The Author

Perry De Fontaine is the founder and president of College Insights, Inc. (www.College-Insights.com), a comprehensive planning firm that specializes in college planning—both financial and admissions. Using a combination of proprietary academic, financial, and tax strategies that are customized to each family's unique situation, College Insights Inc. advises families how to plan and pay for college without going broke. These strategies can potentially save each family thousands—even tens of thousands—of dollars in college costs per year, per student.

In addition to counseling hundreds of families regarding college planning, Perry has conducted numerous seminars for high schools, corporations, and other organizations. He has also been on TV and talk radio, and been quoted in national financial magazines (e.g., *Financial Advisor*) regarding college planning.

Perry is a CPA with over forty years' experience in the financial services industry. Prior to creating College Insights, Inc. in 2001, he was a principal consultant and senior vice president at Willis, the world's third-largest risk management consulting and insurance brokerage firm, and a senior manager at Coopers & Lybrand, directing consulting and audit engagements. Additionally, Perry was a vice president analyzing global financial services companies at Moody's Investors Service and an investment banking senior associate at Salomon Smith Barney, helping clients raise capital and providing mergers and acquisitions advice. He also created and successfully launched the global debt rating service at A.M. Best, the preeminent insurance rating organization. Perry began his career at Continental Corporation, a $10 billion financial services company, where he managed corporate accounting and operations departments and led various complex project teams and task forces.

Perry is passionate about guiding and enabling parents to fund their children's education without risking their own financial stability and future.

Learn more about Perry's work and follow Perry at:

- 🌐 www.college-insights.com
- 🟦 College Insights
- ✖ College Insights
- 🅱 www.getcollegefinancialaid.com

Milton Keynes UK
Ingram Content Group UK Ltd.
UKHW022358220724
445869UK00009B/104